Cambridge Elements

Elements in Ancient East Asia
ENVIRONMENTS: Interaction Zones of Ancient East Asia
INSTITUTIONS: The State and its Military
edited by
Erica Fox Brindley
Pennsylvania State University
Rowan Kimon Flad
Harvard University

INSTITUTIONS AND ENVIRONMENT IN ANCIENT SOUTHERN EAST ASIA (3000 BCE TO 300 CE)

Maxim Korolkov
Heidelberg University

CAMBRIDGE
UNIVERSITY PRESS

Shaftesbury Road, Cambridge CB2 8EA, United Kingdom

One Liberty Plaza, 20th Floor, New York, NY 10006, USA

477 Williamstown Road, Port Melbourne, VIC 3207, Australia

314–321, 3rd Floor, Plot 3, Splendor Forum, Jasola District Centre, New Delhi – 110025, India

103 Penang Road, #05–06/07, Visioncrest Commercial, Singapore 238467

Cambridge University Press is part of Cambridge University Press & Assessment, a department of the University of Cambridge.

We share the University's mission to contribute to society through the pursuit of education, learning and research at the highest international levels of excellence.

www.cambridge.org
Information on this title: www.cambridge.org/9781009507264

DOI: 10.1017/9781108990325

When citing this work, please include a reference to the DOI 10.1017/9781108990325

First published 2024

A catalogue record for this publication is available from the British Library

ISBN 978-1-009-50726-4 Hardback
ISBN 978-1-108-96467-8 Paperback
ISSN 2632-7325 (online)
ISSN 2632-7317 (print)

Institutions and Environment in Ancient Southern East Asia (3000 BCE to 300 CE)

Elements in Ancient East Asia

DOI: 10.1017/9781108990325
First published online: December 2024

Maxim Korolkov
Heidelberg University

Author for correspondence: Maxim Korolkov, maximkorolkov@hushmail.com

Abstract: Over the past decades, archaeological exploration of southern China has shattered the image of primitive indigenous people and their pristine environments. It is known, for example, that East Asia's largest settlements and hydraulic infrastructures in the third millennium BCE were located in the Yangzi valley, as were some of the most sophisticated metallurgical centers of the following millennium. If southern East Asia was not a backward periphery of the Central Plains, then what created the power asymmetry that made possible "China's march toward the Tropics"? What did becoming "Chinese" practically mean for the local populations south of the Yangzi? Why did some of them decide to do so, and what were the alternatives? This Element focuses on the specific ways people in southern East Asia mastered their environment through two forms of cooperation: centralized and intensive, ultimately represented by the states, and decentralized and extensive, exemplified by interaction networks.

Keywords: Southern East Asia, institutions, state formation, networks, environment

ISBNs: 9781009507264 (HB), 9781108964678 (PB), 9781108990325 (OC)
ISSNs: 2632-7325 (online), 2632-7317 (print)

Contents

1 Introduction

Today, southern China – provinces along the Yangzi River and further south – is home to 56 percent of the country's population and about 65 percent of its economic output. This is where wealthy people live: seven of nine provinces with per capita GDP above the national average are in the South. In terms of population, southern China surpassed the Central Plains of the Yellow River valley at some point between the eighth and tenth century CE. By the eighteenth century, the Yangzi and Pearl River Deltas were among the most prosperous regions of the world (Pomeranz 2000; Von Glahn 2016: 322–36).

This is very different from how the South appeared to the early visitors from the Central Plains of north China. The authors of the Warring States (453–221 BCE) and early imperial (221 BCE–220 CE) eras often described it as a wilderness roamed by wild animals, lush with exotic vegetation, and inhabited by primitive people who were incapable of moral self-cultivation and cooperation as a society (Schafer 1967; Brindley 2015). According to this stereotypical account, the demographic and cultural void in the South was filled by industrious Chinese settlers equipped with superior technology and backed by state power.

Over the past decades, archaeological exploration of southern China has shattered this image of primitive indigenous people and their pristine environments. We know, for example, that East Asia's largest settlements and hydraulic infrastructures in the third millennium BCE were located in the Yangzi valley, as were some of the most sophisticated metallurgical centers of the following millennium. Communities in early southern East Asia participated in many overlapping networks of long-distance interaction, which extended far beyond present-day China and did not have a single center. This started to change after ca. 1000 BCE when Sinitic polities occupied ever larger swaths of the Yangzi valley and lands further south. After the mid-first millennium BCE, these polities developed bureaucratic governments, commercialized economies, and intellectual discourses that set them apart from the surrounding groups. In 221 BCE, one of these polities, the state of Qin, unified the Sinosphere into an empire.

If southern East Asia was not a backward periphery of the Central Plains, then what created the power asymmetry that made possible "China's march toward the Tropics" (cf. Wiens 1954)? What did becoming "Chinese" practically mean for the local populations south of the Yangzi? Why did some of them decide to do so, and what were the alternatives? This Element addresses these questions by focusing on the specific ways people in southern East Asia mastered their environment through two forms of cooperation: the first, centralized and intensive, ultimately represented by the states, and the second, decentralized and extensive, exemplified by interaction networks.

1.1 Institutions: States and Networks

People pursue and attain their goals through mastery of their environment achieved through interaction with other people (Mann 1986: 6). The economist Douglass North (1920–2015) defined institutions as "rules of the game" that reduce uncertainty concerning the behavior of other participants in the interaction and make cooperation possible (North 1990: 3). One way to think about institutions is to consider the needs and goals of interacting individuals. Life in early sedentary communities involved two types of cooperation. First, there was intensive cooperation within the community with a high level of commitment by its participants: They had to spend vast amounts of time and energy to sustain artificial landscapes that made their lifeways possible. Second, there was less regular and less intensive coordination over longer distances to secure resources that were not available locally. This type of extensive coordination could also pursue the objective of reducing threats to the community through peaceful resolution of intergroup conflicts.

Intensive cooperation was often achieved through the application or threat of force. The state has been studied as a particularly powerful organizational solution to the coordination problem: an organization created to integrate interests, activities, systems of knowledge, and hierarchies of power in large human groups (Scheidel 2013; Benati and Guerriero 2022). States ensure cooperation within a demarcated territory through centralized administration backed by coercion (Price 1978; Tilly 1990; Vogelsang 2016; Scott 2017). They are at their strongest in mobilizing spatially defined groups for activities that require high levels of commitment, such as warfare (Tilly 1975).

However, centralized and coercive territorial states were not the sole way of intensive cooperation, which could also be achieved when communities shared a sense of overarching order, typically embodied in religious beliefs, and could effectively communicate these ideas (Crone 1989: 129–32; Yoffee 2004: 22–41; Routledge 2014: 27–47). Such hegemonic orders could function in the lack of, or with a minimum of, enforcement and full-time professional administration, and they incurred much less costs for their participants than the full-fledged states. They were also easily dissolvable when participants decided to withdraw (Graeber and Wengrow 2021: 276–327). Such early polities straddle the line between centralized and decentralized cooperation.

Decentralized institutions facilitate low-intensity cooperation across large distances. They complement centralized institutions by making possible acquisition of remote resources that enhance social hierarchies and the coercive capacity of centralized organizations. However, they can also undermine centralized institutions by offering alternative sources of subsistence, wealth, and prestige.

In this Element, heterarchical organizations enabled by such institutions are called "networks." Like the modern global networks, the ancient ones lacked central authority to define the terms of engagement. But the ancients also lacked formal "rules of the game," such as international business laws, financial institutions, measurement standards, or data exchange protocols. In many cases, we do not know exactly how this long-distance cooperation was organized. In other, better-documented contexts, shared elements of material culture – culinary habits, burial customs, or artistic tastes – indicate the circulation of knowledge, human mobility, and exchange of resources and goods (Jennings 2011; Hein 2022; Hudson 2022).

Network cooperation could also feed into polity formation. Many early polities emerged at transregional communication bottlenecks, such as the Nile River valley or the Luoyang Basin, that trapped, directed, and intensified the flows of people, resources, and information (Broodbank 2013: 204–8; M. Li 2018: 175–229). While some of these central nodes disintegrated when their underlying network configurations shifted, they were leaving behind memory communities that could be mobilized in the next cycle of polity building in East Asia (M. Li 2019). The feedback loop between centralized and decentralized cooperation is the central topic of this Element.

1.2 Mastering the Environment Through Settlement, Trade, and Empires

Hominid interference in the environment predates *Homo sapiens*, let alone sedentism and agriculture (Scott 2017: 37–43). After the Middle Holocene (ca. 7000–6000 BCE), high-density settlement and intensive land use opened the way to the systematic replacement of natural ecosystems with those purposefully engineered by humans to capture energy, especially through domesticated plants and animals. These highly productive artificial environments allowed populations to grow and necessitated ever greater labor investments in their maintenance and extension, tying their inhabitants to fixed locations (Brooke 2014; Barnes 2015).

It is at such places that we find the earliest evidence of sustained intensive cooperation by large groups of people. During the fourth and third millennia BCE, farmers along the Yangzi formed communities with populations of thousands and possibly tens of thousands. Southwest of Lake Tai 太湖 (in the north of the present-day Zhejiang Province) they transformed an entire region by constructing dams, water reservoirs, canal networks, and paddy fields (Renfrew and Liu 2018). Around the same time, a millennia-long transition from wetland to farmland started on the Lianghu Plain 兩湖平原 on the Middle

Yangzi (Lander 2022a). Logging of trees around the major population centers may have contributed to the exacerbation of flooding already in the second millennium BCE, although the earliest written evidence of overcutting and overgrazing dates to the mid-first millennium BCE (Lander 2022b; Rawson 2023). It has also been argued that the environmental footprint of these dense agricultural settlements transcended their regional contexts. Ruddiman (2003) hypothesizes that rice farming in the Yangzi Basin released sufficient volumes of greenhouse gases to prevent the global climate from cooling into the next glacial age around 3000 BCE.

Carneiro (1970) famously claimed that the first states appeared among the environmentally circumscribed farming populations, where people had no easy way to escape control. In line with the more recent research on early polities (Wengrow 2010; Graeber and Wengrow 2021), this Element contends that anthropogenic environments of the kind discussed in Sections 3 and 4 involved a variety of cooperation, which was not necessarily enforced by a central authority. Elites, rulers, specialized administrators, and coercion, in different combinations, were present in some places and all but absent in others.

In a longer-term perspective, however, such environments could serve as the building blocks of states, because they provided concentrations of manpower and agricultural production amenable to centralized control and appropriation: the so-called state spaces (Scott 2009). In southern East Asia, several millennia of institutional experiments came to an end with the militarization of cross-regional contacts after ca. 1000 BCE. As discussed in Section 5, during the first millennium BCE, centralized, territorial, and coercive states became the mainstay of social organization in East Asia. Their growth culminated in the third and second centuries BCE when the Qin 秦 and, after its fall, the Han 漢 Empire unified the East Asian ecumene through conquest.

Section 6 shows that empires were ecological projects just as they were military projects. They integrated far-flung territories with diverse environments and used compulsion as well as economic incentives to stimulate exchanges that enriched their elites and intensified resource exploitation. Especially at the early stages of imperialism, this was achieved by violent means, for example, when conquered populations were resettled to new economic heartlands, and hefty tributes were imposed on provinces. In the longer run, empires encouraged transregional trade by reducing military threats, building infrastructures, promoting monetization, disseminating technology, and stimulating consumption (Hopkins 1980; Bang 2008; Morris 2014).

During their heyday between 300 BCE and 300 CE, ancient empires created economic dynamics that left chemical markers for anthropogenic pollution on a global scale. The best-known case is the changing lead levels in the Greenland ice shield that allegedly registered the boom in metal production in the Roman Empire (Brooke 2014: 321–22; McConnel et al. 2018). The state-managed, market-oriented iron industry of the Han Empire might have made a comparable contribution (Lee et al. 2008). The great metropolises of the Warring States and the early imperial era drew on resources far beyond their regions, causing deforestation, soil erosion, and resource extraction on a nearly industrial scale (Duan et al. 1998; Flad 2011: 3). This concentrated demand was made possible by the emergence of new institutions of intensive cooperation and provided a powerful impulse for the expansion of exchange circuits and their appropriation by the states. Ancient empires represented a new type of human organization that enabled more efficient exploitation of the environment by bundling together high levels of power centralization, particularly manifest in coercive capacity, with the extensive geographical outreach of long-distance exchange networks.

1.3 North and South

The Central Plains (see **Figure 1**) have long been an inevitable, if not always articulated, point of reference in any story of social development in southern

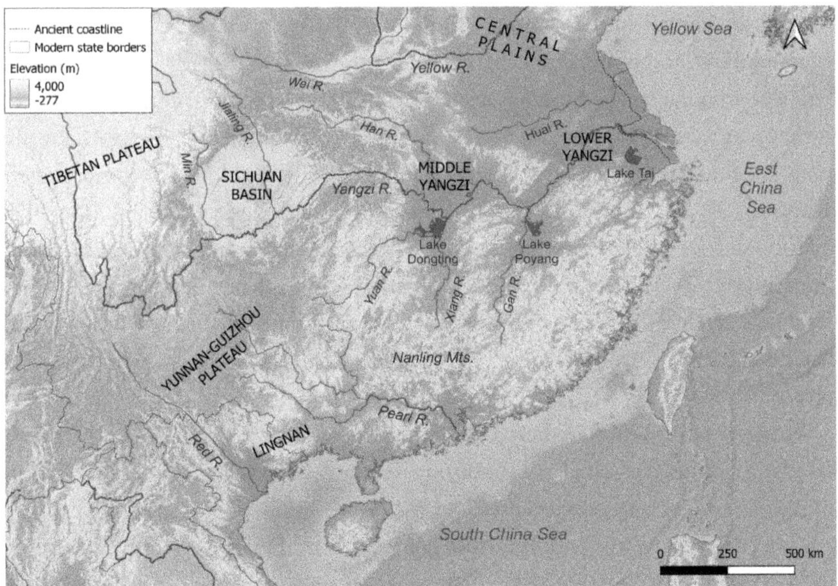

Figure 1 Southern East Asia. Map by the author.

East Asia (for a recent criticism, see Jaffe, Campbell, and Shelach-Lavi 2022). When archaeologist Zhang Guangzhi 張光直 (Kwang-chih Chang, 1931–2001) developed his Chinese Interaction Sphere model, he sought to highlight the contributions of continental East Asian Neolithic cultures outside the Central Plains to the formation of Chinese civilization. The role of the Central Plains was all too clear, while the significance of other regions had to be demonstrated (Chang 2006). To the scholars studying the fourth- and third-millennium BCE walled city at Liangzhu 良渚 or the remains of early copper smelting on the Middle Yangzi, these finds signal the cultural sophistication of people previously thought to have been dependent on the Central Plains for their social and technological development (Guo 2013; Renfrew and Liu 2018; Liu, Qin, and Zhuang 2020; Chen 2022).

Applying the Central Plains yardstick to the societies of southern East Asia forces the verdict of the latter's civilizational underperformance that accrued through the early Bronze Age and became decisive around the turn of the first millennium BCE. Ian Morris' "measures of social development" – settlement size, energy capture, information technology, and war-making capacity – are not precision instruments, especially when it comes to prehistoric and early historic societies (Morris 2003), but they do highlight important shifts. During the Late Neolithic, the largest settlements in the Yangzi valley were larger than those in the north, and they remained comparable at the beginning of the Bronze Age (see Section 4). However, by the end of the second millennium, the Shang capital at Anyang 安陽, north of the Lower Yellow River, was by far the greatest population center in East Asia, both in terms of area and the number of inhabitants (Campbell 2018). Moreover, its elites had access to information and war-making tools beyond the reach of their southern counterparts: the military technology from the northern steppes, of which war chariots are the most spectacular but not the sole element, and a full-fledged writing system (Rawson 2015; Campbell 2018; Rawson, Huan, and Taylor 2021). The writing-and-weapons complex enabled central rulers to communicate and enforce decisions on a scale previously impossible. It was instrumental when the Zhou leaders took the intensive cooperation in East Asia to a new level around 1000 BCE by forging the first unambivalently transregional polity in this part of the world.

As early as the late fourth and third millennium BCE, some communities in the Yangzi valley were using elaborate systems of graphs to inscribe pottery and stone objects, none of which, so far as we know, developed into proper writing, defined as a set of symbols for recording language (Qiu 2000; F. Li 2018; Demattè 2022: 99–223). Likewise, some of these people were up to speed with the latest military technology (excluding chariots), but the scale of intercommunal violence most likely fell far short of the Shang and Zhou levels (Campbell 2014b; Campbell 2018). As a result, transregional polities did not emerge. It appears that some societies in southern East Asia had necessary technical prerequisites yet did not scale up centralization, administration, and coercion, or at least did not do so as consistently as the societies in the Central Plains.

Archaeologist Yoshinori Yasuda (2013b) famously, if controversially, contrasted the peaceful "civilization of beauty and compassion" created by the rice farmers of southern East Asia to the expansive, dryland agriculturalist and pastoralist "civilization of force and conflict" in northern China. The former was allegedly less prone to geographical expansion and resulting intercommunal conflict because its high-yield rice agriculture supported population packaging, while the latter was in permanent search of more land to plant its less productive millets (Qin and Fuller 2019).

Although, as we will see in Section 3, early rice farmers were not necessarily as averse to mobility as this theory claims, Li Min (2018: 83–95) makes the point that starting from the third millennium BCE, communities in northern China developed more extensive and consequential cross-regional connections than their contemporaries in the lowlands to the southeast. Inner Asia, including the highlands on the northwestern fringes of the Central Plains, was more exposed to colder and drier conditions that set in toward the end of the third millennium. Climate change contributed to population mobility within the Eurasian steppe and forest belt, which involved the domestication of horses and camels as well as increased use of wheeled transport. At the same time, the eastward spread of bronze metallurgy across Eurasia made metal prospecting, mining, and exchange of metals important factors of long-distance connectivity (Anthony 2007; Kohl 2007; Brooke 2014; M. Li 2018). The rapid spread, around the turn of the second millennium BCE, of the Seima-Turbino technological tradition, which allowed the casting of close-combat-effective socketed bronze weapons, attests to the militarization of northern Eurasian networks. In the following centuries, these networks facilitated the equally swift transmission of other revolutionary military innovations, including chariots and mounted horseback riding (Novozhenov 2012; Jaang 2015; Rawson, Huan, and Taylor 2021).

Lieberman's (2008) juxtaposition of exposed zones and protected rimlands of medieval Eurasia can be applied to the institutional divergence of northern and southern East Asia from the early Bronze Age onward. The North's continuous exposure to superior military technologies of the Inner Asian steppe zone favored centralized military command, geographically extensive mobilization of war-related expertise (weapon-casting, horse-breeding, chariot-making), and inter-polity competition. According to Tainter (1988: 124–26), such competition generated energy subsidies for the victors that reinvested the resources of vanquished rivals in increasingly complex centralized institutions. In contrast, societies of southern East Asia were insulated from the direct military challenge of the Steppe until the age of the Mongol conquests. As a result, they lacked the impetus for perpetuating centralization and had more room for social experimentation, which is traced in this Element. It also contends that, despite having been cut short by the expansion of Sinitic states from the north in the first millennium BCE, the institutional diversity and dynamism of ancient southern East Asia had a lasting impact on Chinese and world history.

2 Southern East Asia: Geographical and Environmental Orientations

Southern East Asia is a roughly triangular geographical zone bordered by the Yangzi River in the north, the Tibetan Plateau in the west, and the Pacific Ocean in the southeast (see **Figure 1**). The land surface slopes down from the west to the east. The highlands of the western Sichuan and Yunnan-Guizhou Plateau (Southwestern Highlands) at the eastern fringe of the Tibetan Plateau are a vast mountainous region with floor elevations ranging between 3,000 and 500 m above sea level. It includes some large alluvial basins, such as the Dian Lake 滇池 Basin in central Yunnan. East of the highlands lies the hilly belt with an average elevation of 250–500 m crisscrossed by mountain ridges rising above 2,000 m. This belt stretches from the Sichuan Basin in the northwest to Guangxi and Guangdong in the southeast. Finally, there are the eastern lowlands of the Middle and Lower Yangzi, Lower Pearl River, and Lower Red River valleys, most of which lie below the elevation of 50 m.

Mountains and rivers define the physiographic division of southern East Asia. The Yangzi valley comprises three regions that, starting in the Neolithic, saw the emergence of complex societies and highly productive farming. These are the Sichuan Basin, the Middle Yangzi, and the Lower Yangzi. In the south, the Nanling Mountains 南嶺 separate the Yangzi from the Pearl River drainage. The region south of the mountains is historically known as Lingnan 嶺南 (Ch. "south of the [Nanling] Mountains"), which encompasses the Pearl and Red River systems separated by the hilly country that hinders overland communication. The key feature of all these regions is the presence of a large plain surrounded by a hilly periphery: the Chengdu Plain 成都平原 in Sichuan, the Lianghu Plain in the Middle Yangzi, the Lower Yangzi Plain, and the Pearl and Red River deltaic plains. The two other zones, on the contrary, are the uplands traversed by narrow river valleys: the Yunnan-Guizhou Plateau and the Southeastern Hills of the present-day southern Zhejiang and Fujian Provinces of China.

The divide between northern and southern East Asia is climatic rather than topographic. The Central Plains of northern China have a temperate climate with cold winters, warm to hot summers, and relatively low annual precipitation. Southern East Asia belongs to subtropical and tropical zones with hot, humid summers and relatively warm winters. The climate here is shaped by the East Asian monsoon that pulls the masses of warm, moist air from the Western Pacific into the low-pressure zone over the Tibetan Plateau during the summer. As the oceanic air rises and cools over the continent, it releases heavy rainfall. Warm temperatures and abundant precipitation in summer months make possible wet rice cultivation. Today, rice is the key agricultural crop south of the Yangzi. When one crosses the river and travels northward, one soon finds oneself in the rice–wheat borderland, where the two crops are equally represented, and then arrives in the dryland agricultural zone of north China (Talhelm et al. 2014). Of course, there is considerable climatic variability within the territory as big as southern East Asia, especially between its highland and lowland regions.

The ecology and environment of southern East Asia, as we know them today, formed through the natural and anthropogenic processes during the Holocene, or post-glacial period (ca. 10000 BCE to present). The natural processes were by far more important in the period considered in this Element, but the human-driven changes become increasingly pronounced. The Holocene is characterized by fluctuations between cool/dry and warm/humid conditions. As the ice shields in the northern hemisphere melted during the warm periods of 8500–7000 BCE and 6000–3000 BCE, the ocean rose to its modern level, which reduced the gradient of rivers, slowed their flow, and accelerated sedimentation processes (Roberts 1989: 87–126; Brooke 2014: 114–204). Filling in of the Paleo Lake Yunmeng 雲夢 in the Middle Yangzi created the Lianghu Plain (Lander 2022a), home to some of the earliest and largest walled sites in East Asia. Deltaic plain formation along the Lower Yangzi, Peal, and Red Rivers continued well into the historical period, but human interventions became a significant factor after the end of the period considered here (Marks 2004: 53–83; Li 2015). Another crucial process was the weakening of the East Asian monsoon after the mid-Holocene transition (5000–3000 BCE), leading to a cooler and drier climate in north China and enhancing the north–south divide in East Asia (Clift and Plum 2008: 211–16; Marks 2012: 19). As we will see in Section 3, the Pacific monsoon fluctuations have been used to explain the expansion and contraction of settlement and the fate of the Late Neolithic civilizations of the Yangzi valley.

2.1 Interregional Connectivity

The poem “Lady of the Xiang River,” ascribed to the famous ancient poet Qu Yuan 屈原 (ca. 340–278 BCE), describes an imaginary boat journey through the borderlands of the state of Chu 楚 south of the Middle Yangzi (Owen 1996: 157–58). The dense network of navigable rivers defined interregional connections in southern East Asia. On the eastern coast, seafaring developed as early as the Late Neolithic. In the Southwestern Highlands, where the stream gradient is too steep for the rivers to be navigable, people could travel on foot along the river valleys across the mountains. On long-distance journeys, travelers had to switch between foot and boat.

We can think of connectivity across southern East Asia in terms of key transportation corridors, three of them running roughly in the east–west direction, and three from north to south (see **Figure 2**). The first three are the principal rivers of the region, the Yangzi, Pearl, and Red Rivers, that connect the western highlands with the coastal plains in the east. Three longitudinal corridors are organized around various features of the terrain. The western corridor runs along the rim of the Tibetan Plateau. At its northern terminus, mountain passes east of the Min Mountains 岷山 connect the Sichuan Basin to the Hexi Corridor 河西走廊, one of East Asia’s principal gateways to Inner Eurasia. The corridor proceeds along the mountain ridges south of the Sichuan Basin into the Yunnan-Guizhou Plateau, where it adjoins

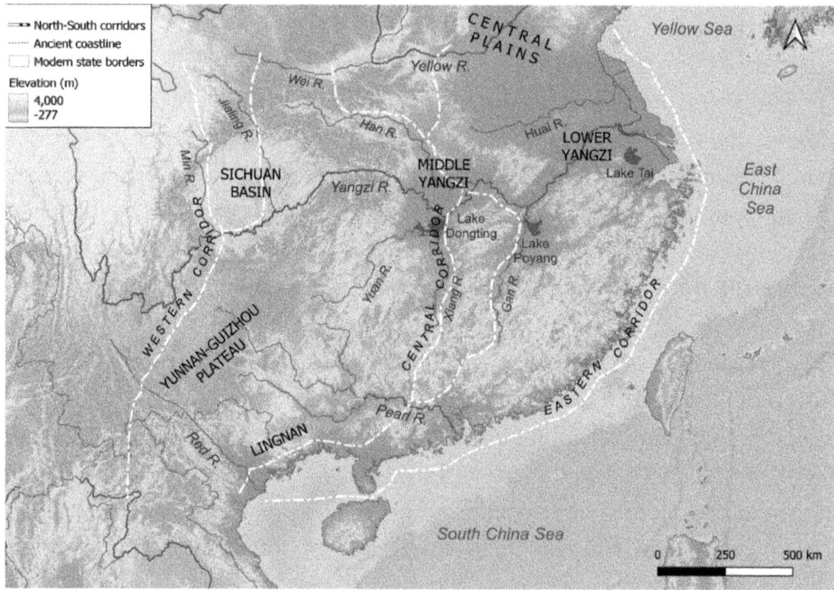

Figure 2 Communication corridors in southern East Asia. Map by the author.

the two east–west corridors: the Pearl and the Red Rivers. To the west of the Plateau, Jinsha (e.g., the upper course of the Yangzi), Mekong, and Salween Rivers run roughly parallel to one another for over 300 km in the so-called Three Parallel Rivers area. The Mekong and Salween valleys are the Southeast Asian extension of the western corridor. Scholars have argued that this route served the spread of millet agriculture and, later, bronze metallurgy from the Upper Yellow River across Sichuan and Yunnan to Vietnam and Thailand (Sørensen 1972; Higham 2021).

The central corridor is formed by the northern and southern tributaries of the Middle Yangzi. The northern tributary, the Han River 漢水, flows from northwest to southeast through the Hanzhong 漢中 Basin and is joined by its northern tributary, the Tangbai River 唐白河, which traverses the Nanyang 南陽 Basin in southwestern Henan. These are the portals between the Yangzi valley and the Central Plains of North China. Through the Nanyang Basin, one enters the floodplain of the Lower Yellow River Basin, and from Hanzhong, the Wei River 渭河 valley, which in the late first millennium BCE became the heartland of the Qin and Han Empires. The southern section of the corridor leads to the Nanling ridges along the Xiang River 湘江 valley south of Lake Dongting 洞庭湖 and the Gan River 贛江 valley south of Lake Poyang 鄱陽湖. After crossing the Nanling mountain passes, travelers find themselves in the northern tributary valleys of the Pearl River. In preparation for his campaign in Lingnan in 214 BCE, the First Emperor of Qin ordered the construction of the Ling Canal 靈渠 across the Yangzi–Pearl River watershed, which created the all-water route from the Central Plains to the tropical Far South (Lin 2017: 99–130).

The eastern corridor made use of the coastal waters of the Yellow, East China, and South China Seas. Populations associated with the Hemudu 河姆渡 culture (ca. 5500–3300 BCE) south of Hangzhou Bay were familiar with rowing boats (Underhill and Habu 2006; Qin and Fuller 2019), and the Late Neolithic communities in the Min River 閩江 estuary in the present-day Fujian Province heavily relied on marine resources. By 3000 BCE, some of these people were so expert in seafaring that they crossed the 180-km-wide Taiwan Strait and settled on the island. Archaeological finds attest to the cross-strait movement of basalt, ceramic, and stone tools, and hint at the possibility of cabotage navigation along the coast of Guangdong between the Pearl and Red River estuaries (Rolett et al. 2011; Li 2019). Although it is unlikely that any single boat made it all the way from the Yangzi Delta to northern Vietnam, the coastal corridor was important for migrations and cultural exchanges from the Late Neolithic onward (Higham 2019). With the emergence and expansion of polities, this world of offshore islands and maritime mobility became a refuge from the state power, as metaphorically illustrated in the popular stories about the First Emperor's failure to reach the mythical isles of the immortals in the Eastern Sea (Sima 2006: 6.247).

2.2 Early Agriculture and Farmer Migrations

Around 3000 BCE, southern East Asia was home to a variety of multi-resource subsistence regimes that combined hunting, gathering, fishing, and food production, including plant cultivation and animal husbandry. By 300 CE, the vast majority of the region's population relied on cereal farming for their livelihood. Particularly important was wet rice, one of the most labor-intensive crops to cultivate. The development of productive economies, and the social institutions that accompanied them, set in motion migrations, exchanges, and emulations that lay down the pathways for the subsequent expansion of trade networks, territorial states, and empires.

As elsewhere in the world, people in southern East Asia engaged in plant cultivation as one of many subsistence strategies aimed at exploiting specific niches in the dynamic ecology of the early and Middle Holocene. Wild rice prospers at the margins of seasonally flooding lakes and rivers. These wetlands, which extended farther north during the early Holocene climatic optimum than they do nowadays, are among the most biologically diverse ecosystems. As such, they were favored by hunter-gatherer groups, whose earliest engagement with rice may have started as far back as 11000 BCE (Qin and Fuller 2019). The data for the early farming communities in East Asia around 6000–5000 BCE indicates that consumption of cereals provided between 15 percent and 25 percent of food intake (Barnes 2015; Stevens and Fuller 2017). On the ecotones (transition areas between biological communities) such as coastal plains and river estuaries, humans adapted to the changing sea levels, precipitation, and temperature regime by switching between food production and foraging well after the emergence of full-fledged cereal agriculture (Higham 2019). Even in the established farming communities, wild plants and animals remained crucial to subsistence until the Late Neolithic (Barnes 2015).

Domestication of plants, defined by morphological changes that made plants dependent on humans for their reproduction, marked the crucial transition in early cultivation. Concomitant increase in grain size reinforced human–plant symbiosis by making rice and other domesticates more attractive partners for humans. In southern East Asia, the domestication of rice occurred in the Lower and Middle Yangzi valley in the fourth millennium BCE (Fuller, Qin, and Harvey 2008). At one of the sites south of the Yangzi Delta, Caoxieshan 草鞋山, rice grains constitute 70 percent of plant remains. From this time on, farming also came to involve heretofore unseen labor investments, including the construction of the earliest known paddy fields (Barnes 2015; Qin and Fuller 2019).

These new lifestyles created the basis for intensive and extensive cooperation discussed in this Element. Most immediately, Neolithic agricultural intensification greatly increased the carrying capacity of land and allowed more concentrated populations, which required much more sophisticated coordination than before. According to a recent calculation, based on conservative assumptions, a self-sufficient community of wet rice farmers could have up to 14,000 inhabitants, while millet agriculture could support groups of up to 2,000 people (Qin and Fuller 2019). These enormous (by hunter-gatherer standards) populations branched out into the surrounding areas and created extensive interaction networks. The language-farming dispersal hypothesis argues that the outward migrations of farming groups explain the geographical spread of most modern language families (Sagart 2005; Bellwood 2013: 123–39; Higham 2021).

Qin and Fuller (2019) believe that this model requires modification. They pointed out that, by responding with increased yields to an extra investment of labor, wet rice agriculture supported population packing rather than spatial expansion. In contrast, millet and rainfed (dryland) rice cultivation, which was much less productive per unit of land, pushed populations outward in search of more land. This means that wet rice-based communities, such as those in the Lower Yangzi valley, are unlikely to expand out of their home region. In most of the Yangzi Basin, however, variable and vertical topography necessitated crop diversification if the farmer communities were to make use of the entire range of available ecologies. Other paramount East Asian cultivars, foxtail, and broomcorn millets were introduced from North China to the Middle Yangzi and Sichuan in the fourth millennium BCE and became an essential part of "a perfect packet for agricultural expansion" (d'Alpoim Guedes 2011; Nasu 2012).

The spread of farming was part and parcel not only of the early interregional contacts but also of the later state expansion. Agrarian historian James C. Scott coined the term "state spaces" for specific geographies that favored the concentration of grain production and manpower and thereby facilitated centralized control and appropriation (Scott 2009). As we will see in Sections 5 and 6, territorial states and empires in East Asia expanded by incorporating the emerging state spaces, although their ability to tap various agricultural systems was uneven.

2.3 Metals as Connectivity Drivers

Metal ores are unevenly distributed across East Asia. Major copper deposits are located along the Middle and Lower Yangzi and in Yunnan, as well as in southern

Shanxi and Gansu Provinces in north and northwest China. Tin ores are concentrated south of the Yangzi River, in the present-day provinces of Yunnan, Guangxi, Guangdong, Hunan, and Jiangxi. Tin is scarce in north China, except for Inner Mongolia. Lead is more widely distributed, but about 64 percent of China's deposits are in the afore-mentioned southern provinces as well as in Gansu and Inner Mongolia. Copper and tin mines in southern China are part of the greater metal belt that extends into Southeast Asia (Higham et al. 2020). What made the Yangzi copper zone particularly important for early metallurgists is that most of its ore deposits occurred on the surface or were shallowly buried, which facilitated mining (Liu and Chen 2003: 37–44).

The development of copper metallurgy in Eurasia by the fourth millennium BCE, and especially the subsequent transition to multi-metal bronze alloys, created a powerful stimulus for long-distance connectivity (Vandkilde 2016; Hudson 2022: 1–4). Metallurgical knowledge was probably introduced to East Asia from Central Asia and South Siberia in the third millennium BCE (Jaang 2015). From their early bases in the Hexi Corridor, highland prospectors advanced into the Yangzi copper belt through the western corridor and reached Middle Yangzi by the early second millennium BCE (M. Li 2018: 108). By1000 BCE, another wave of metallurgist migration reached the Southwestern Highlands, leaving behind the earliest bronze-casting sites in Yunnan (Chiou-Peng 2009). Higham (2021) suggested that these people moved in search of new sources of copper and tin to satisfy the demand of the expanding metal industries in the Central Plains, Sichuan, and on the Middle Yangzi (see Section 4). Studies of lead isotope data point to northeastern Yunnan as a possible source of highly radiogenic lead ores used by the Shang and early Western Zhou foundries in the late second millennium BCE (Jin et al. 2017; Liu et al. 2018).

Bronze Age states often followed in the wake of metallurgists. The recent analysis of trace elements in copper groups identified in the early Chinese bronze objects reveals the trend toward centralized procurement and distribution of metals after the foundation of powerful polities such as Western Zhou, and the geographic extension of their supply networks (Li et al. 2020; Hsu et al. 2021). However, well into the second half of the first millennium BCE, state access to the major metal regions in the Yangzi valley had to be negotiated with the local mining communities rather than administered directly (Wu 2022).

3 Agricultural Expansion, Social Complexity, and Polity Formation, 3000–1800 BCE

Around the year 3000 BCE, human effort was transforming the landscapes along the Yangzi River. Some communities made themselves highly visible through monumental architecture. Massive earthen ramparts that enclosed an area of hundreds of hectares sprang up across the Chengdu Plain in Sichuan, along the edge of the Middle Yangzi wetland, and south of the delta. Some of these settlements probably had populations in the tens of thousands. Together, they formed regional networks that shared food-serving customs, domestic architecture, religious beliefs, communal celebration practices, and other behaviors. To present-day archaeologists, these networks are known as archaeological cultures: Baodun 寶墩 in the western Sichuan Basin, Qujialing 屈家嶺-Shijiahe 石家河 in the Middle Yangzi, and Liangzhu south of the Yangzi Delta (**Figure 3**).

Some of these societies had elites who controlled wealth and labor and engaged in elaborate rituals. In other regions, hierarchies were less articulate. But in all cases, large groups of people were able to develop centralized institutions that facilitated intensive coordination of labor and resources. According to one estimate, the construction of a city wall of one major center north of the Middle Yangzi would have kept 1,000 laborers busy for ten years, while another 20,000–40,000 farmers would have been needed to supply them with food (Nakamura 1997).

The simultaneous upscaling of intensive social coordination in the Upper, Middle, and Lower Yangzi valley, the three regions that had limited connections to each other in this early period, calls for an explanation through an independent variable, such as climate change. Brooke (2014: 175–83) argued

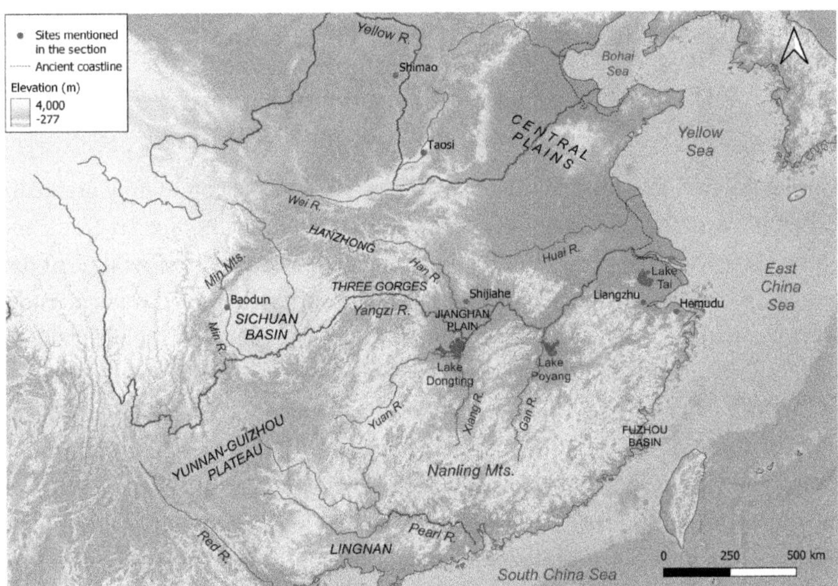

Figure 3 Southern East Asia in the Late Neolithic. Map by the author.

that across the Old World, the rise of states stemmed from economic intensification, rationalization of group leadership, and enhancement of collective memory through writing and monumental symbolism. All of these were responses to the Mid-Holocene climatic crisis, which intensified in 3200–2900 BCE. The climate in the northern hemisphere shifted toward cold and dry conditions punctuated by an erratic interchange of extreme aridity and precipitation. However, the evidence for the late fourth millennium BCE East Asia is muted at best. Abrupt fluctuations in rainfall and sea levels appear to have played a more significant role in the crisis of Late Neolithic civilizations of the Yangzi valley around 2000 BCE than in their rise some thousand years earlier.

Another problem with sweeping explanations is that they gloss over the differences between the regions in question, which can be as significant as similarities. The massive walls of Baodun, Shijiahe, and Liangzhu may have been their most visible features, but the three societies varied in their ecological conditions, demography, and political organization. While wet rice was the dominant crop in the Yangzi Delta, communities in the Middle Yangzi and Sichuan combined it with millet agriculture, which was introduced from outside their regions, as was also the rice in the case of Sichuan. As discussed in the previous section, the composition of the agricultural package defined farmers' ability to exploit diverse ecological niches, expand geographically, and develop transregional networks. It was also central to the settlement patterns. As a result, societies in the three regions developed different institutions that shaped their subsequent trajectories.

3.1 The Heyday of Centralization and Hierarchy South of the Yangzi Delta: Liangzhu

During the fifth and fourth millennia BCE, a new kind of community gradually crystallized in the seasonally flooded wetlands south of the Yangzi Delta and along Hangzhou Bay. People still relied on a diverse package of wild plant and animal resources. Aquatic plants such as water caltrop, lotus, and water chestnut were particularly important, as were marine species, including shellfish. But an increasingly greater amount of labor was invested in the production and storage of wet rice. Sites of the Hemudu Culture (ca. 5100–3300 BCE) on the coastal plain of northern Zhejiang Province included paddy fields, irrigation ditches and wells, and storage pits. To prepare these fields, people armed themselves with new instruments: Some 170 spade-like tools made of bone were excavated at Hemudu, even though recent research suggested only half of them were used to dig soil (Xie et al. 2017). Tool production might have been a factor of craft specialization during this period. Another one was the growing architectural complexity of settlements. Hemudu and other contemporaneous sites yielded the remains of multistoried wooden dwellings on stilts, fragments of a paved pathway, and even a 15-m-long log bridge between the residential area and the surrounding rice fields. A new mortuary tradition, which centered on large burial platforms made of layers of soil and pebbles and developed in the Lower Yangzi valley in the fourth millennium BCE, also involved labor organization on a new scale (Sun Guoping 2013; Shelach-Lavi 2015: 103–23; Derevyanko 2016: 185–91).

Reliance on rice farming led to more investment in fixed infrastructure, which enhanced agricultural productivity in a positive feedback loop, particularly powerful in the case of labor-intensive wet rice agriculture. These processes propelled sedentism to new levels. While no population numbers are available for Hemudu communities, the discovery of about twenty tons of rice husks at the Hemudu site (Shelach-Lavi 2015: 117) points to the centralized collection, storing, and distribution of grain reserves among the population that came to depend on this crop (Barnes 2015: 122).

Around the year 3000 BCE, the gradual intensification of sedentism, agriculture, and redistributive institutions exploded into what many scholars consider the earliest state in East Asia (Renfrew and Liu 2018; Childs-Johnson and Major 2023: 20–48). A huge walled settlement emerged in the area called Liangzhu south of Lake Tai, centered on the trapezoid mound of layered clay and sand 7 m high and with an area of 30 ha, probably a palatial foundation. The space enclosed by the walls was about ten times larger, and residential and production areas outside the ramparts occupied an area of up to 800 ha. The population could have exceeded 60,000 people (Liu, Wang, and Chen 2020).

Surrounded by a network of smaller towns and villages, Liangzhu City presided over the first region-wide artificial landscape transformation in the Yangzi valley (**Figure 4**). Around 2900 BCE, eleven dams were erected north and northwest of the city. The largest one ran along the Dazhe Mountain slope for a length of 5 km. It had a width between 20 m and 50 m and a height of 2–7 m and was built of earthen blocks wrapped in grass and bamboo. A series of smaller dams further upstream of the mountain river prevented seasonal monsoon floodings and conserved water for irrigation in several reservoirs with a total capacity of about 60 million m^3. By one estimate, the construction of the largest levee required the labor of 3,000 people working for eight years to move 2.88 million m^3 of earth. The whole hydraulic system functioned as a coherent whole, suggesting central planning (M. Li 2018: 43–59; Liu et al. 2018; Liu, Wang, and Chen 2020).

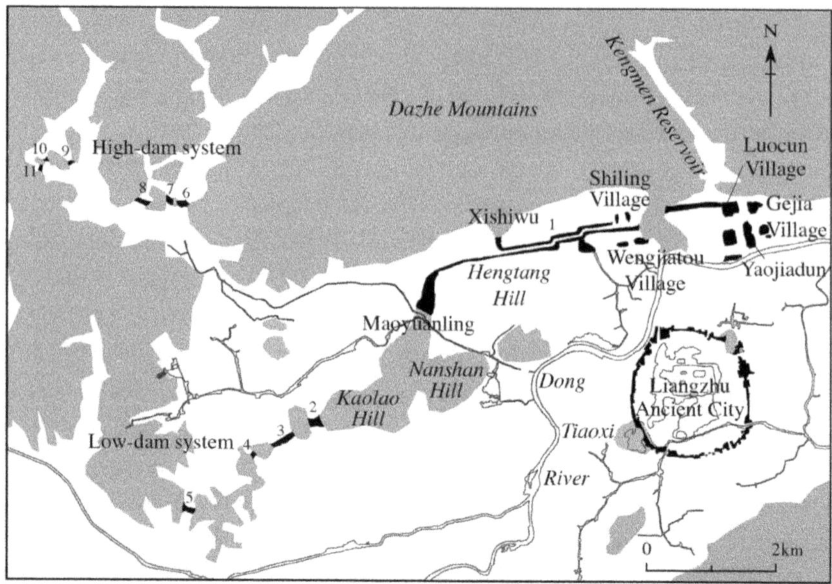

Figure 4 Artificial hydraulic landscape in the Late Neolithic: Liangzhu and its environs. Source: Renfrew, C., and Liu, B. (2018). The emergence of complex society in China: the case of Liangzhu. *Antiquity*, 92, 975–990.

The new regime of centralized labor management reshaped the countryside. At the Maoshan 茅山 site, the patchwork of small, irregularly shaped paddy fields was after ca. 2800 BCE replaced by a large-scale, rectangular grid formed by well-designed, carefully constructed paths and irrigated by the canals (Zhuang, Ding, and French 2014; Qin and Fuller 2019). Intensified rice agriculture generated considerable surpluses, which were stored at the palatial platform at the center of Liangzhu: Archaeologists excavated thirteen tons of carbonized rice from one of the storage pits (Liu, Wang, and Chen 2020).

About 200 m northwest of the palatial mound, another artificial platform, known as Fanshan 反山, served as a necropolis for people who controlled much of the wealth, labor, and technical knowledge in the Liangzhu society. Strict north–south orientation and uniform placement of grave goods in eleven tombs arrayed in two parallel rows reveal a highly standardized mortuary ritual. Funerary assemblages centered on hundreds of exquisite jade objects, including such new forms as *cong* cylinders, which may have been used as staff heads, as well as jade discs and trapezoid plaques with an image probably representing a major deity or deified deceased rulers. This repertoire and iconography were shared across the elite cemeteries in the Lower Yangzi region. Jade battleaxes in the tomb of a paramount leader buried at the Fanshan mound highlight the importance of ritualized violence in the construction of social power at Liangzhu (M. Li 2018:

49–52; Renfrew and Liu 2018; Rawson 2023: 11–15). Comparison with the commoner cemetery at Miaoqian 廟前, about 6 km east of the city, reveals a vast wealth gap with the elites: a typical commoner tomb contained but a small number of ceramic pots, tripods, and stemmed cups, while some also included tools and small jades, such as beads (Qin 2013; Derevyanko 2016: 382–83).

Liangzhu elites oversaw the highly specialized production of exquisite jades, lacquer, silk, and ceramics, which were distributed throughout the region, probably in exchange for food and raw materials. Some innovations during this period point to the growing importance of communication, including the dense web of artificial and natural waterways that connected Liangzhu to the Yangzi River, and an elaborate system of graphs on pottery and stone objects, which was shared by the communities across the delta (Deopik and Ulyanov 2011; Zhang 2015; F. Li 2018; Demattè 2022: 169–93).

3.2 Walled Towns on the Middle Yangzi: Qujialing-Shijiahe

The Middle Yangzi was among the earliest centers of sedentism, agriculture, and pottery production in southern East Asia. In the Li River 澧水 valley northwest of Lake Dongting, rice domestication was underway as early as 7500–6000 BCE. The remains of a paddy field at the site of Chengtoushan 城頭山 (fifth millennium BCE) may well be the earliest rice paddy ever discovered (Pei 2013). This is also one of the earliest fortified settlements in East Asia, with a walled area of approximately 10 ha (Yasuda 2013a). During the Daxi 大溪 Culture period (ca. 4300–3300 BCE), Chengtoushan became part of a cluster of settlements, some of which were separated by less than 2 km. Another such cluster emerged on the western fringe of the Jianghan Plain 江漢平原 north of the Yangzi; as the river sediments gradually filled in the wetland from the northwest, the riverbed moved south, and the walled settlements spread from the hillsides into the alluvial plain (Pei 2020: 97–124). The walls may have been primarily used as flood control barriers rather than defense from human enemies, and they were probably also useful in keeping wild animals away (Priewe 2012; Lander 2022a; Liu 2023).

The strength of the East Asian monsoon affected the water level in Lake Dongting, which defined human habitation in the Middle Yangzi throughout the Neolithic. According to Liu et al. (2011), Neolithic settlement migrated basin-wide in response to the waxing and waning of the lake, spreading into the lowland south of the Yangzi riverbed when the water retreated in the Daxi period, and regrouping north of the river when the lake area expanded in the subsequent Qujialing period (ca. 3300–2600). By the beginning of the third millennium BCE, new walled towns sprang up across the Jianghan Plain (Flad and Chen 2013: 116–18).

A regional survey northwest of Wuhan points to significant changes in the settlement distribution around 3000 BCE when the population increased from several hundred to 5,000–14,000 people. Most of them came to dwell in two walled towns, Taojiahu 陶家湖 and Xiaocheng 笑城, where population density approximated that of present-day New York City. Sturm (2017) suggested this transition involved the emergence of some kind of centralized leadership in Qujialing communities to enable coordination in such large and dense populations. Even these are dwarfed by the eponymous settlement of Shijiahe Culture (ca. 2600–2000 BCE) with a walled core of 120 ha and a settlement area of some 8 square km. By various estimates, between 10,000 and 50,000 people lived here. They were served by sophisticated public facilities, such as drainage systems with ceramic pipes. Along with the massive walls, moats, dykes, and embankments, this infrastructure suggests a considerable degree of planning and community integration (Flad and Chen 2013: 120–22; Zhang 2013).

Shijiahe was the largest settlement in the network of more than twenty walled towns on the Lianghu Plain, which shared layout features and communal ceremonies. Institutions of intensive cooperation in these communities strikingly differed from those of Liangzhu. Burials in the Shijiahe Culture region show a much lower level of wealth differentiation, and there is no sign of religious leadership or the significance of violence for the construction of an elite persona. Social cohesion appears to have been based on communal rituals, including libations that left behind a deposit of some hundred thousand drinking cups just at one locus in Shijiahe. Other ceremonies involved the use and burial of thousands of clay figurines of domestic and wild animals (pigs, dogs, sheep, tigers, elephants), humans, and structures, which are among the most recognizable items of Shijiahe Culture (**Figure 5**). Their numbers and distribution suggest inclusive ritual activities open to much of the Shijiahe population, and probably also to the people from the surrounding countryside (Flad and Chen 2013: 120; Shelach-Lavi 2015: 158).

Guo and Sturm (2022) write about the "collective ethos" of Qujialing-Shijiahe society, cultivated through shared labor, community participation, and a connection to the landscape. As the climate became drier after 2500 BCE, populations moved outside the walled towns into lower-lying lands, which suggests a considerable degree of adaptivity to the changing environment in the lack of compulsion to keep the population together within the circumscribed state spaces. The walled centers continued to be used as loci of ritualized, broad-based community-building.

Figure 5 Ceramic figurines from Shijiahe. Source: Wikimedia Commons.

These activities may also have played a role in the regional integration. Guo (2013) describes three urban clusters within the Qujialing-Shijiahe Culture space as confederations that participated in shared rituals and probably joined forces in large-scale construction projects. It has also been argued that the Shijiahe walled towns were ritual centers par excellence, and the Shijiahe network developed around religious institutions such as annual festivals, which attracted participants from outside the Middle Yangzi region (Ehrich 2017; M. Li 2018: 65–66).

3.3 Sichuan Crossroads: Baodun

Late Neolithic civilizations of the Lower and Middle Yangzi valley developed from indigenous sedentary societies that thrived for millennia before the ramparts of Liangzhu and Shijiahe were erected. In contrast, the development of walled towns on the Chengdu Plain in the third millennium BCE was from the beginning embedded in long-distance interactions of the highland Western Corridor. The Chengdu Plain was sparsely occupied when the first Baodun Culture (ca. 2700–1700 BCE) settlements sprang up along its western edge. However, north and northwest of the Sichuan Basin, archaeologists discovered more than 100 sites associated with the Majiayao 馬家窯 Culture (ca. 3300–2500 BCE) of eastern Gansu, with its distinctive painted pottery. It appears that by the early third millennium BCE, migrants from the north settled the Upper Min 岷江 and Jialing River 嘉陵江 valleys before descending into the Chengdu Plain around 2700 BCE (Flad 2013; Flad and Chen 2013: 81; M. Li 2018: 149–52). They brought along dryland millet agriculture and pig husbandry. Only gradually did these people adapt rice into their subsistence package (D'Alpoim Guedes 2011).

The reason these people were slow to step into the plain probably has to do with the unpredictable and violent floodings of the Min River as it fans out of the Min Mountains (Flad 2013). According to Zeng et al. (2016), they finally moved south when the cooling in the northwestern plateaus and simultaneous drying of the swampy land in the Chengdu Plain created the necessary combination of push and pull factors. However, the risk of floods never subsided completely, especially as the settlement expanded into the interior of the plain. Communities responded with innovations in settlement architecture. While the functions of Qujialing-Shijiahe walls are still debated, scholars agree that those of the Baodun Culture sites primarily served flood prevention (Flad 2013; Zeng et al. 2016).

Baodun is the largest of nine Baodun Culture walled towns that have been identified so far. It consists of inner and outer enclosures with areas of 66 ha and 220 ha. Flad and Chen (2013: 84) estimate that the inner wall of Baodun could have been built by 4,000 people working hard for a month. Its construction involved an organized collective effort and represents "an important integrative practice common among Baodun communities." North of Baodun, the walls of the second largest settlement, Yufucun 魚鳧村, enclosed an area of 40 ha and were built of alternating layers of clay and cobblestone – the structure also observed at other Baodun sites – in a one-time construction event (Y. Wang 2003). The Baodun towns also share ceramic assemblages and a style of residential architecture: the above-ground wattle-and-daub houses (Flad 2013).

Tombs excavated at the Baodun Culture sites offer no signs of wealth stratification and the presence of elites and political leadership. Rather, it seems that the coordination needed for efficient flood control provided the principal impetus for communal integration. Ritual activities may have also played their part, as suggested by a large platform at the center of the Gucheng 古城 site, with what can be interpreted as the remains of stone altars (Flad and Chen 2013). The spread of rice agriculture during the Baodun period (Zeng et al. 2016) should have necessitated more cooperation in water management and the construction of paddy fields. However, throughout their history, Baodun communities continued to diversify their food resources, which allowed greater settlement mobility and opportunity to regroup in the new environmental conditions. Such a diversification shaped the long-distance connections of Baodun populations and their response to the crisis that marked the first turning point in the history of complex societies in southern East Asia.

3.4 Expansion and Transregional Networks

Interactions along the transregional communication corridors intensified with the increase in settlement size and density along the Yangzi River. The underlying factors included outmigration from areas of high population density and the quest for resources to supply these populations and their industries. In later times, polities instrumentalized human migrations in the interests of their rulers and elites, but for the period considered in this section (3000–1800 BCE), such institutions are difficult to trace because of the lack of written records.

The nonmetric cranial data, as well as dental and mitochondrial DNA data from the burial sites in coastal Southeast Asia, along with the changes in funerary customs, stone tools, and the evidence for rice cultivation and pig husbandry, indicate migrations from the Yangzi valley after ca. 2000 BCE. According to Higham (2014, 2019, 2021), farmer groups sailed southwest along the coast from the Yangzi Delta, settling the Fuzhou 福州 Basin around 3000–2300 BCE and influencing the material culture of the Late Neolithic communities on the Guangdong coast (Li 2019). An alternative point of view claims the central role in the southward spread of farming for the Middle Yangzi and the central riverine corridor across the present-day Hunan and Jiangxi Provinces, from where some of the migrants entered Fujian (Deng et al. 2018; Dai et al. 2021).

In the west, farmers from the Sichuan Basin, equipped with the rice-millet system of the Baodun Culture, advanced into the Southwestern Highlands at the end of the third and the early second millennium BCE. At the sites they left behind, crop remains reached over 86 percent of the plant assemblage (Dal Martello 2020). Moving down the Salween valley, farming groups reached the Khorat Plateau in northeast Thailand by the nineteenth century BCE (Higham 2021). More agriculturalists may have infiltrated the highlands from the northeast: Several settlements associated with the Qujialing-Shijiahe Culture were identified in the Yuan River 沅江 valley that provided upstream access from the Middle Yangzi to the Yunnan-Guizhou Plateau (Korolkov 2022: 40).

We do not have a definite answer to the question about the kind of connections, if any, that these migrants maintained with their former homelands, nor are we certain about how they contributed to transregional integration. The extent of resource-procurement networks of the early urban centers on the Yangzi was rather limited: For example, the diagnostic ritual regalia of the Liangzhu Culture were crafted from the local jade (Liu 2003). Yet, the discovery of Liangzhu-style jades and ceramics at the locations between the Lower Huai River 淮河 in the north and the Pearl River Delta in the south indicate the broad circulation of material items and, according to some scholars, religious and political ideas that defined the membership in the Liangzhu world (M. Li 2018: 54–56).

Similarly, the clay figurines and red cups central to the communal ceremonies in the Qujialing-Shijiahe walled towns are found at many contemporary sites north of the Yangzi, where the Han River provided a corridor of north–south communication. Many of these objects were probably imported from the Middle Yangzi centers, and, according to Priewe (2012), at least some of their users were likely aware of their original ritual contexts. Spanning the Yellow River, Huai, and Yangzi valleys, this network facilitated the multidirectional spread of beliefs and customs, as in the case of urn burials introduced to the Middle Yangzi from Shandong and Anhui (Priewe 2012; M. Li 2018: 65).

Although the organizational aspects of this connectivity remain obscure, its participants circulated technical knowledge with far-reaching implications for the communities in southern East Asia. The presence of copper ore and slag at the sites of the Late Shijiahe Culture (ca. 2000 BCE) has been sometimes interpreted as evidence of a precocious, indigenous Bronze Age culture (Guo 2013: 48). The earliest presence of copper ore and slag at the sites of Late Shijiahe Culture (ca. 2000 BCE) coincides with the appearance of Shijiahe objects at the pioneering bronze casting centers in north China, such as Taosi 陶寺 (in Shanxi Province) and Shimao 石峁 (in Shaanxi Province) (Priewe 2018; Jaffe, Campbell, and Shelach-Lavi 2022). A plausible scenario is that the early metallurgists "piggybacked" on the preexisting transregional networks.

3.5 Collapse or Reconfiguration?

The abrupt decline of the walled centers in the Yangzi valley around 2000 BCE has been related to the so-called –4.2 k BP (before the present) event: a climate change that involved cooling air temperatures, disastrous droughts, and sharply dropping water levels in rivers and lakes. It is best documented in the Mediterranean, southwest Asia, and parts of east Africa, and is believed to have caused the collapse of the Early Bronze Age polities, including the Akkadian Empire and the Old Kingdom in Egypt (Dalfes, Kukla, and Weiss 1997; Brooke 2014: 282–85). The East Asian record is more ambiguous, suggesting volatility in precipitation that led to alternating floods and droughts (Flad and Chen 2013: 124). Some recent studies argue against sweeping environmental explanations of shifts in subsistence and settlement systems at the end of the third millennium BCE (Jaffe and Hein 2021). Shelach-Lavi (2018a) pointed out that a dramatic decrease in population densities and complexity occurred primarily on the seaboard, while the evidence for the areas removed from the coast is much more mixed.

The Yangzi Delta provides the clearest case of an environmental upheaval leading to the demise of a Late Neolithic civilization. Speleothem (mineral deposit) records from two caves in the region indicate the onset of a drought after ca. 2400 BCE punctuated by two pulses of severe pluvial conditions that left sediment layers covering the Liangzhu site. The second episode terminated the human occupation of Liangzhu around 2300 BCE. The subsequent Qianshanyang 錢山漾-Guangfulin 廣富林 Culture lacked the population density and the technological sophistication of Liangzhu. These later communities succumbed to a massive drought around 2000 BCE, leaving the lands south of the Yangzi Delta largely deserted (Zhang et al. 2021). The most centralized and elitist society in the Yangzi valley presents the case of the most thorough collapse.

Middle Yangzi also experienced large-scale depopulation and abandonment of all of its major walled sites at the end of the third millennium. However, around 2000 BCE the largest of them, Shijiahe, was reoccupied by a group that developed an original jade carving tradition and a far-flung exchange network, which possibly extended as far north as the Central Plains (Priewe 2018) and provided a context for the beginnings of copper mining in the region. Smaller settlements associated with the Shijiahe Culture survived in the Yuan River valley southwest of Lake Dongting (Korolkov 2022: 40). In the east of Jianghan Plain, the site of Panlongcheng 盤龍城 was already populated in the third millennium and became the principal center on the Middle Yangzi during the transition to the Bronze Age (1800–1300 BCE). Despite its cultural connections to the Central Plains (see Section 4), Panlongcheng likely hosted some of the Shijiahe populations that regrouped in a new settlement pattern after 2000 BCE (Guo 2013: 46–47).

The Baodun Culture communities in the Chengdu Plain were equally used to settlement relocation in response to ecological change. Having moved into the alluvial plain and adopted rice cultivation in the third millennium, they resettled back into areas of higher elevation during the Late Baodun period (2000–1700 BCE), probably to confront increasing floods. The proportion of rice in the plant assemblages decreased by half, and some wetland weeds disappeared completely, while millets, legumes, and fruit became better represented, indicating a swing toward a dryland agricultural regime (Zeng et al. 2016). Although most of the walled sites were deserted, some stayed occupied, most notably, Sanxingdui 三星堆, which was about to become the center of one of the most idiosyncratic Bronze Age cultures of southern East Asia (Xu 2006; H. Sun 2013; Campbell 2014a: 54–55).

Two climatic transitions – the Mid-Holocene crisis and the –4.2 k BP event – have been used to explain the growth and collapse of sedentary communities and their interaction networks in the Yangzi valley. More recent research reveals considerable sociocultural continuities in most of the Yangzi regions across both purported divides. It also highlights a variety of institutional solutions to the challenges of rising population density and coordination over long distances in the contexts of migration and the quest for resources.

Some societies, such as Liangzhu, produced powerful elites that planned and oversaw region-wide man-made landscape transformations unparalleled in East Asia until the advent of the Iron Age in the second half of the first millennium BCE. They also created lasting emblems of authority that continued to be rediscovered and used throughout China's history (Shelach-Lavi 2018b; Childs-Johnson 2019). Other societies, such as Qujialing-Shijiahe and Baodun, coordinated their large-scale projects around broad-based ritual activities in the lack of self-aggrandizing leaders. It is tempting to correlate these diverging institutional strategies to how the societies fared through the climatic instability of the late third millennium BCE, but such arguments cannot be pushed too far. The severity of the crisis varied from region to region, its impact was probably strongest at the coast, and it is unclear if a less centralized institutional package would have improved the fate of Liangzhu.

Southward farmer migrations from the Yangzi valley, some of which span off the population movements that originated further north, shaped the geography of long-distance interactions in southeastern Eurasia, including the directions of subsequent migrations and the exchange routes for prestige goods, mineral resources, and animals (Higham 2021). While we know next to nothing about how such geographical knowledge was transferred over distances and across generations, continuity in transregional networks of human mobility, exchanges, and information played a crucial role in the spread of metallurgy in southern East Asia after 1800 BCE.

4 Joining the Eurasian Bronze Age, 1800–1000 BCE

Copper-base metallurgy developed in western Eurasia in the late fifth and fourth millennium BCE and was transmitted eastward during the third millennium (Kohl 2007). Metal-yielding sites appeared in China's northwestern Gansu Provinces after 3000 BCE, and their number increased considerably toward the end of the third and early second millennium BCE when lead-tin bronzes and the remains of metallurgical production are attested at the sites of Qijia 齊家 (ca. 2200–1600 BCE) and Siba 四壩 (ca. 1900–1500 BCE) cultures (Mei 2009; Jaang 2015). The precise routes of transmission remain debated. Contrary to the assumption of Western transmission, bronze-yielding sites in the Gansu Corridor are dated earlier than in Xinjiang to the west. Alternative routes may have run across southern Siberia and Mongolia (Mei 2003; Linduff 2018).

At the end of the third millennium, metallurgy reached the Central Plains of north China as part of a broader package of objects, technologies, and subsistence resources exchanged within the northern Eurasian interaction sphere. Metallurgists at Taosi and Shimao used Inner Eurasian methods of one-piece open mold and bivalve mold casting (Jaang 2015; M. Li 2018: 95–115). Then, in the first half of the second millennium BCE, the workshops at Erlitou 二里頭, the largest settlement in the Lower Yellow River valley at that time (**Figure 6**), developed piece-mold bronze production, which required a complex division of labor, managerial organization, and accumulation of resources in the large, elite-controlled foundries. This new method was used to cast increasingly large bronze vessels used in the royal and elite rituals, which became the signature artifacts of the Chinese Bronze Age (Bagley 1999; Liu and Chen 2012: 271–72). This was a radical departure from the Eurasian tradition of small, family-level bronze production centered on personal ornaments, weapons, and tools.

As pointed out in Section 2.3, the quest for metal ores was driving transregional connectivity during the Bronze Age. Liu and Chen (2003: 75–79) interpreted the presence of Erlitou-type ceramics at some Middle Yangzi sites as evidence of Erlitou state expansion into the Yangzi copper belt. More recently, scholars paid attention to the highly selective adoption of Central

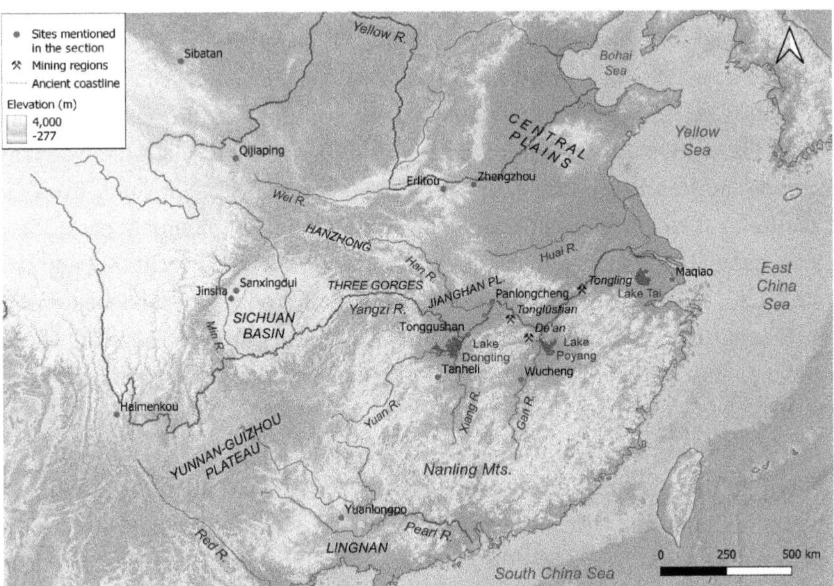

Figure 6 Southern East Asia in the early Bronze Age. Map by the author.

Plains-style pottery by the local populations and emphasized that the nature of interactions underlying these influences is unclear (Campbell 2014a: 60–61; Shelach-Lavi 2015: 189–90). Yet, the beginning of copper mining in the Middle and Lower Yangzi was clearly influenced by the demand if not of the dynastic centers in the North, then of the local foundries, many of which were modeled on the Central Plains prototypes. Equally consequential was the circulation of resources, technology, and material repertoires among the communities along the Yangzi and further to the south.

In the Central Plains, the onset of metallurgy is woven into the narrative of state formation, as bronze vessels and weapons provided elites with more potent symbols of power and tools of coercion, while metal production required centralization of manpower, resources, and management (Liu and Chen 2003; Li 2013: 41–65). In southern East Asia, too, the early Bronze Age was the time of regeneration of centralized institutions after their relative decline during the transition period around 2000 BCE. However, due to a combination of environmental and institutional factors, neither of the Yangzi-based centers succeeded in taking the state power to the next level and creating a multiregional polity like the one that emerged in North China at the very end of the second millennium BCE.

4.1 Stepping into the Bronze Age

To supply its vigorous bronze casting, turquoise, jade, ceramic, and probably also textile and lacquer industries and to secure massive volumes of timber and stone needed for constructing its palace-temple complex, Erlitou expanded its resource networks far beyond its heartland in the Luoyang Basin. Some of its population settled along the communication corridors. In the south, the sites with Erlitou-style ceramics dot the route from Luoyang through the Nanyang Basin to the Han River valley. Other routes proceeded straight south from the Huai River Basin through the Tongbai 桐柏-Dabie 大别 mountain passes into the Jianghan Plain and southeast into the Lower Yangzi (Pang 2018; Pang and Gao 2020). It is unclear if the appearance of small bronze tools and weapons at the Maqiao 馬橋 Culture (ca. 1700–1300 BCE) sites around Lake Tai, in the former Liangzhu homeland (Campbell 2014a), was due to these contacts, but the distinctive Central Plains tradition of piece-mold casting did not spread outside Erlitou during this period.

Despite the attempts to draw a connection between the Erlitou expansion and the collapse of Shijiahe (Xiang 2011), there is little to suggest any kind of northern conquest of the Middle Yangzi valley in the first half of the second millennium BCE. However, around the middle of the millennium, a major center with an unambiguous Central Plains connection emerged in the Yangzi valley. Panlongcheng was not an entirely new settlement. This site in the east of the Shijiahe Culture sphere remained populated through the early second-millennium hiatus and the Erlitou period, but it was radically transformed after 1500 BCE. A powerful earthen citadel enclosing an area of 7.5 ha and surrounded by a moat was built in the middle of a 100-ha area that included houses, workshops, and cemeteries. A 1-m-high rammed-earth platform in the northeast corner of the citadel carried the foundations of three large buildings oriented 20 degrees east of north (Bagley 1999; Flad and Chen 2013; Campbell 2014a).

The use of a rammed-earth construction technique, distinct palatial complexes, and cardinal orientation of the Panlongcheng citadel and its public buildings have no antecedents on the Middle Yangzi, but they have close parallels at Zhengzhou 鄭州, which became the capital of a new Central Plains polity after the decline of Erlitou. With its inner walls surrounding an area of almost 300 ha and the outer walls, roughly 13 km^2, this was by far the largest city East Asia had seen by that time. The rapid spread and wide geographical distribution of the Erligang 二里崗 ceramic tradition (named after the location in the modern city of Zhengzhou where this culture has first been identified), settlement and building orientation, and bronze inventory are sometimes interpreted as evidence for "Erligang empire" (Wang 2014; Zhang 2020). Others, however, have pointed out that "the actual relationships between sites [of the Erligang Culture] and the mechanisms of putative control remain unknown" and that they were "likely indirect, mutable, and based on ritually reinforced kinship hierarchy, alliance and sporadic rather than routine mechanisms of coercion" (Campbell 2018: 64).

At Lijiazui 李家嘴, just outside Panlongcheng's eastern wall, two elite tombs dated to between 1500 and 1400 BCE stick to the Erligang funerary protocol: rectangular shaft with a terrace in the middle and a sacrificial pit at the bottom, painted wooden chamber with inner and outer coffins, and human victims laid atop the outer coffin or terrace (Bagley 1999; Steinke 2014). On the other hand, poorer tombs at Yangjiawan 楊家灣 cemetery north of the citadel mostly do not fit into the Erligang mortuary syntax. The ceramic tradition at Panlongcheng is typologically continuous with the local Late Neolithic, shares ornamental patterns of the Middle and Lower Yangzi ceramics, and includes a high proportion of high-fired stoneware (often called "primitive porcelain" or "protoporcelain"), a distinctive product of the Yangzi kilns (Needham, Kerr, and Wood 2004: 132–35). Far from representing a wholesale replacement of the local population by the conquering northerners, Panlongcheng was probably home to some Zhengzhou elite émigrés. According to Campbell (2014a), "Erligang royal control over Panlongcheng, if ever actually direct, may have been fluctuating and contingent on regional politics and shifting alliances among high elites." Panlongcheng's role as a copper-procuring outpost of the Erligang state has also been questioned in recent studies that revealed differences in the isotopic profile of metals and the composition of alloys used at Zhengzhou and Panlongcheng (Liu et al. 2019).

Be they the lieutenants of the kings in far-away Zhengzhou, renegade northern aristocrats, or local chiefs who adopted Erligang-style rituals and patronized emigrant metallurgists, powerful individuals such as those buried at Lijiazui introduced a technology with enormous consequences for regional and transregional connections: bronze metallurgy. Miners who, around 1500 BCE, built the earliest known shafts at Tonglüshan 銅綠山, one of the principal copper regions in the Yangzi valley, most likely supplied metal ores to the Panlongcheng foundries some 100 km northwest. Materials of the "Panlongcheng horizon" have also been found at Tongling 銅陵, another major mining area in the present-day Anhui Province, and at De'an 德安 tin mines west of Lake Poyang in Jiangxi Province (Liu and Chen 2001; Wu 2022). Panlongcheng ceramic tradition reached its maximum distribution along the Middle Yangzi after ca. 1400 BCE, at the time when the Erligang capital in the north was largely abandoned (Campbell 2014a: 115).

The Panlongcheng elites and craftsmen introduced the Central Plains piece-mold casting of ritual bronze vessels to the Yangzi valley, but they were not the only vector of southward transmission of metallurgical knowledge. The scarce metal repertoire of the Maqiao communities in the Lake Tai Basin, which may predate Zhengzhou and Panlongcheng, was probably produced with the help of the Eurasian techniques of open and bivalve casting in small workshops (Huan 2023: 101–6). At the opposite end of southern East Asia, the site of Haimenkou 海門口 in northwestern Yunnan, dated between the thirteenth and eleventh centuries BCE, yielded twenty-six copper and bronze objects, mainly small tools such as adzes, awls, socketed chisels, and fishhooks, as well as personal ornaments and one half of a bivalve mold used to cast some of these items. Other finds at the site, including double-handed painted pottery and the earliest remains of wheat and barley in the Southwestern Highlands, point to the connections with the Middle and Upper Yellow River valley along the eastern edge of the Tibetan Plateau (Chiou-Peng 2009; Dal Martello 2020). Chiou-Peng (1998) suggested that these innovations were brought about by the late second millennium BCE migrations of farmer-and-pastoralist populations of northwestern China that came to be known as the Qiang in the latter Chinese texts.

These small groups of bronze specialists, who traveled and were buried with the tools of their trade – molds, crucibles, ceramic chimneys – moved along the mountain valleys and river corridors, spreading their craft, prospecting metal deposits, and bringing ever more far-flung regions into the Eurasian Bronze Age network. By the late second millennium BCE, these people were smelting copper in eastern Lingnan, and they buried six sandstone bivalve molds and at least thirty fragments of broken ones at a large cemetery at Yuanlongpo 元龍坡 in central Guangxi. From there, or possibly from central Yunnan via the Red River corridor, the small-scale bronze industry spread into northern Vietnam. Around 1000 BCE, copper-producing sites appeared in the Khao Wong Prachan valley of central Thailand, where the migrants, possibly coming from Yunnan along the Salween River, repopulated the settlements abandoned in Late Neolithic (Ciarla 2007; Higham et al. 2011; Higham 2014: 131–95; Higham et al. 2020; Higham 2021).

The Central Plains and the Eurasian bronze traditions were not geographically separated. Along with the large, elite-controlled workshops, the early Bronze Age centers such as Zhengzhou also had family-operated foundries casting weapons, tools, and ornaments for private users. These small craftsmen may well have been the vectors of metallurgy transmission into southern East Asia. At the same time, the resource- and labor-intensive elite tradition of the Central Plains had revolutionizing effects on social, political, and economic centralization. However, the actual outcomes in southern East Asia were different from those in the dynastic polities of the Central Plains, and they also varied from region to region.

4.2 Indigenous Bronze Age Centers on the Yangzi River

Panlongcheng was abandoned at some point between 1400 and 1300 BCE. Why and how this happened is somewhat of a mystery: The site shows no traces of violent destruction or disastrous flooding. The end of Panlongcheng coincided with a general crisis in the Erligang world. Its center at Zhengzhou was depopulated, and its residents partly relocated north of the Yellow River (Liu and Chen 2003: 98–99). On the Middle Yangzi, too, the geographical spread of Panlongcheng ceramic assemblage in 1400–1250 BCE suggests that the Panlongcheng population dispersed to new locations, amalgamating with the local groups, spreading their metallurgical skills, and opening new mines south of the Yangzi. Bronze-casting sites sprang up east and west of Lake Dongting (Campbell 2014a: 161–63; McNeal 2014). In the following centuries, some of them became the foci of indigenous polity formation and joined the emergent network of the Yangzi-based bronze-using societies.

The presence of Erligang-style ceramics at the early (ca. 1400–1250 BCE) layers of the Tonggushan 銅鼓山 site northeast of Lake Dongting may point to the initial presence of a migrant group from Panlongcheng, but local pottery prevails at the latter Anyang-period (ca. 1250–1050 BCE) layers. A string of bronze-producing settlements stretched along the eastern and southern edges of the lake into the Lower Xiang River valley. The largest of these sites discovered so far is Tanheli 炭河里, dated to the last centuries of the second and the beginning of the first millennium BCE. It is located on the northern bank of the Huangcai River 黃材河, a western tributary of the Xiang, and overlooks a small valley. The town was surrounded by a circular wall built of clay and pebble stones, in marked difference to the Central Plains rammed-earth technique attested at Panlongcheng. The remains of what has been interpreted as palatial buildings, and the likely presence of a bronze foundry and a jade workshop, suggest that Tanheli might have been the center of a moderate-sized polity, the rulers of which had access to costly materials, complex technology, and specialized workers (Hunan sheng wenwu kaogu yanjiusuo, Changsha shi kaogu yanjiusuo, & Ningxiang xian wenwu 2006; Yu 2013; Lai 2019: 22–23).

If the scale of metallurgy at Tanheli remains unclear, other bronze founders in the Dongting region had fully mastered the Central Plains piece-mold casting by the final centuries of the second millennium. They put it to use to produce an array of objects, including the wine-serving vessels of metropolitan Shang types, but also specifically local sets of *nao* bells, the largest of which weighs 220 kg, far heavier than contemporaneous bells from the Shang capital at Anyang (Bagley 1999; Lai 2019: 70–73). Unlike in the North, where bronzes are prominently featured in the funerary context, the Hunan bronzes have often been recovered from pits located on hills and near rivers. To Gao (1984), this suggests the worshipping of nature spirits, accompanied by the performance of bell music and the offering of vessels filled with small ornaments of jade and bronze. As we will see shortly, the elements of this ritual culture were shared by other societies in the Yangzi valley, one manifestation of a thickening cross-regional network of interactions.

East of the Lianghu Plain, the Lake Poyang region straddles the border of the Middle and Lower Yangzi valley. The copper resources of the nearby Tongling mines were probably known to the Panlongcheng metallurgists. By the middle of the second millennium BCE, the settlement was expanding in the Lower Gan River valley south of Poyang, and their inhabitants interacted with Panlongcheng and other Erligang Culture centers north of the Yangzi, as well as with the Maqiao Culture groups around Lake Tai in the Yangzi Delta. Local potters took stoneware manufacturing to a new level. Their high-fired, glazed ceramics was coveted by elite consumers as far north as Zhengzhou (Sun 2003;

Wang 2019). Here, at thc fringe of the Erligang sphere and the intersection of multiple exchange networks, one of the principal centers of southern East Asia's Bronze Age emerged around 1530 BCE.

The pentagonal citadel at Wucheng 吳城, on the western bank of Gan River about 150 km southwest of Lake Poyang, encloses an area of over 60 ha. Its massive earthen walls, some sections of which are 60 m wide at the base, were constructed within a short period at the beginning of the site occupation. The city was divided into specialized areas. The ritual zone on one of the five hills within the settlement centered on a large red-earth platform with the remains of pole structures. Residential quarters include semi-subterranean houses, wells, pits, and drainage ditches. The discovery of fourteen ceramic kilns with sloping firing tunnels and multiple firing chambers attest to the role of Wucheng as an important supplier of "protoporcelain" wares, while the finds of many casting molds and fragments, along with the locally produced bronze vessels, tools, and weapons, illustrate the operation of a large, indigenous metallurgical center. Wucheng potters marked their products with signs that possibly represent a yet undeciphered script with similarities to the contemporary oracle bone inscriptions of the Late Shang and the incised graphs of the Maqiao Culture in the Lower Yangzi (Jiangxi sheng wenwu kaogu yanjiusuo and Zhangshu shi bowuguan 2005; Demattè 2022: 239–43).

About 20 km east of Wucheng, on the opposite bank of the Gan River, the burial at Dayangzhou 大洋洲 in Xin'gan 新淦 county, dated to ca. 1200–1100 BCE, contains one of the richest bronze assemblages ever discovered in China: 54 vessels and bells and over 400 tools and weapons, along with 150 jades and 356 pieces of pottery, including high-fired protoporcelain ceramics. While some bronzes were probably imported from the north, the bulk of the metal artifacts represent the local manufacturing and cultural traditions. The elite individual buried at Dayangzhou had no use for wine-serving and drinking vessels favored by his counterparts at the contemporaneous metropolis of the Central Plains, the capital of the Shang state at Anyang. Also, in contrast to the Late Shang, human sacrifices do not appear to have played an important role in Dayangzhou (Jiangxi sheng wenwu kaogu yanjiusuo, Jiangxi sheng bowuguan, and Xin'gan xian bowuguan 1997; Bagley 1999; Steinke 2014).

Bagley (1999) concludes that Wucheng and Dayangzhou "are clearly the remains of a local power, a city and the cemetery of its rulers." At the peak of its geographical extension around 1200 BCE, the Wucheng Culture sites appeared in the upper reaches of the Gan River, and Wucheng-associated groups probably crossed the Nanling Mountains into Lingnan (Laptev 2011). However, toward the end of the second millennium BCE, Wucheng suffered violent destruction, probably at the hands of a competing neighboring polity with its center at

Niucheng 牛城, east of the Gan River. It has been suggested that the occupant of the Dayangzhou tomb was the leader not of Wucheng but of this new regional power, which endured into the early first millennium BCE (Jiangxi sheng wenwu kaogu yanjiusuo and Zhangshu shi bowuguan 2005).

Unlike other major Baodun Culture settlements on the alluvial plains of the western Sichuan Basin, Sanxingdui survived the climatic tribulations of the early second millennium. Its rise as the regional center was possibly due to the eastward movement of populations from the flood-troubled Min River valley to the more hydraulically stable Yazi 鴨子河 valley (Wan 2020). Sanxingdui's expansion after 1750 BCE involved the construction of a 7,800-m-long rammed-earth wall, 40 m thick at the base, that enclosed an area of some 260 ha. According to Flad and Chen (2013: 92), the labor invested in this wall was several times greater than at most of the largest Baodun Culture sites. The building remains include small above-ground wattle-and-daub houses that probably served as residences for the general population, as well as large buildings in the northern part of the site that possibly served as palaces and shrines. Such public structures are not attested at the earlier settlements in the Sichuan Basin and, along with other evidence, have been interpreted as the markers of the emerging centralized authority (Song 2008; Flad and Chen 2013: 91–92; Sun 2013).

Sanxingdui owes its worldwide fame to two sacrificial pits discovered in 1986. They belonged to a large ritual area in the southwestern part of the site, where six more pits were excavated in 2019–2020. These pits are residues of sacrificial activities that took place shortly before the abandonment of Sanxingdui around 1200–1100 BCE and involved the deliberate breaking and burning of bronze, jade, and gold ritual objects and other artifacts, many of which might have been previously used in the shrine ceremonies (Zhao 2022a). Many items are unique and have ever since been widely celebrated as the legacy of a mysterious civilization strikingly distinct from the Bronze Age of the Central Plains. Human-like bronze heads, some of which "wear" golden masks; a full-sized human figure in bronze; bronze altars; and 4-m-high bronze trees belonged to a "world that figured in ritual and religion" (Sanxingdui Museum 2006; Rawson 2023: 93–116).

However, a closer analysis of sacrificial pits highlighted a far-reaching web of external connections, rather than an isolated, idiosyncratic culture. Sanxingdui metallurgists used piece-mold casting probably introduced from the Central Plains as early as the Erlitou period, and the Erligang motifs in the bronze ornaments point to continuing contacts with the Shang metropolitan workshops. These connections were mediated by the new bronze-casting centers that arose in the Middle Yangzi and Upper Han River (Hanzhong) valleys in the latter half of the second millennium BCE. In parallel to the Hunan region, people at Sanxingdui used alcohol vessels as containers for cowrie shells that ultimately originated in the Maldives Islands in the Indian Ocean (Yang 2019: 1–19). Many of the liquid containers excavated from the Sanxingdui pits were probably produced in the Hunan workshops (Bagley 1999; Lai 2019: 52). The images of human-avian hybrids invite comparisons with Dayangzhou. The numerous finds of *yazhang* 牙璋 jade scepters indicate Sanxingdui's engagement in the western highland networks, where these objects played a prominent role in rituals since the Late Neolithic (Falkenhausen 2006b; M. Li 2018: 187–89; Zhao 2022b; Rawson 2023: 112–13).

Sanxingdui's extensive resource and technology networks, a well-integrated system of specialized craft production, especially bronze casting and jade carving, and the ceremonial symbols of violence, such as the jade dagger-axes, set it apart from the earlier Baodun Culture centers and point to the presence of political leadership. Based on the analysis of the hairstyles of sixty-five bronze figures from two sacrificial pits, Sun Hua (2013) identified two elite groups of ritual and administrative specialists, which composed the ruling class of the Sanxingdui polity. Although more cautious in their interpretations, Flad and Chen (2013: 93–94) also observe "a relative shift in the importance of individuals in society" and "a degree of network strategizing (defined as political actions that are exclusionary and individually centered . . .) in the political aspect of Sanxingdui society that is not evident in Baodun Culture remains."

4.3 Strengthening Interactions in Southern East Asia

The spread of metallurgy across the Yangzi valley after ca. 1400 BCE created a new dynamic of cross-regional interaction and political centralization. Migrations of Erligang-associated elites and craftsmen may have played an important role in the Middle Yangzi, while in the case of Sichuan, technology was likely transmitted by the still poorly understood groups in the Three Gorges and Hanzhong (Falkenhausen 2006b; Rawson 2023: 110–12). During the following centuries, populations of the new bronze-producing centers pushed the prospecting, mining, and metal trading frontiers south of the Yangzi and into the highlands southwest of the Sichuan Basin. The compositional and isotope studies on the ancient bronze artifacts indicate that metal sources – some probably as far away as the present-day Yunnan Province – were shared by the major Yangzi-based foundries, which formed a basin-wide network of metal circulation (Campbell 2014a: 179; Pollard et al. 2017; Chen et al. 2019; Liu et al. 2019).

The movement of metals created a new interaction framework in southern East Asia, but the elites of Wucheng, Tanheli, and Sanxingdui mobilized a far broader range of resources – jade, ivory, gold, cowrie shells, fine ceramics – to display status and project authority. Alongside the renewed construction of defensive walls and palatial buildings, authority centralization was reignited by the need to manage a large, specialized labor force and control the flow of materials necessary for casting massive bronze objects: vessels from the Dayangzhou tomb near Wucheng, bells from sacrificial pits in Hunan, and human figures and trees at Sanxingdui shrines. These items were deployed in new, cross-regional religious practices that enlisted the support of supernatural forces for communities and their leaders. One such practice was pyromancy, a form of divination that applied heat to animal bones (including turtle shells) to produce future-telling cracks. It was introduced to the Yangzi Basin from north China during this period and became a potent tool of authority legitimization (Flad 2008; Shelach-Lavi 2015: 254–57).

The trans-local acquisition of material and immaterial resources strengthened the circulation of ideas and wealth. The geographical distribution of decorative elements, such as tiger imagery, and specific types of objects, such as human-like bronze faces excavated at Hanzhong, Xin'gan, and Sanxingdui, points to the shared cults or, at least, communication of motifs and religious concepts across the regional borders. The finds of bronze bells in sacrificial pits in the present-day provinces of Hunan, Hubei, Anhui, Jiangxi, Jiangsu, Zhejiang, and Fujian mapped the distinctive sphere of "southern" rituals centering the performance of music on the riverside or in the hills, probably to please nature spirits (Bagley 1999; Falkenhausen 2006b; Campbell 2014a: 115; Lai 2019: 78–80). Likewise, the use of bronze containers and bells for storing cowrie shells and small jade ornaments suggests the development of a shared ritual practice among the Yangzi-based societies, which spread further south in the first millennium BCE (Shelach-Lavi 2015: 253; Yao 2016).

The early Bronze Age in southern East Asia saw a rise in intercommunal violence, likely precipitated by population growth and conflicts over metals and other resources. Evinced in the destruction of Wucheng and images of prisoners from the site of Jinsha 金沙 in the Chengdu Plain (Wang 2019; Rawson 2023: 115), it may have contributed to the southward migrations from the Yangzi valley. Laptev (2011) opines that Wucheng emigrants disseminated metallurgy south of the Nanling Mountains between 1200 and 1000 BCE. Contacts along the Xiang River corridor may explain the burying of bronze vessels in nonfunerary pits in the early first millennium BCE Lingnan, which parallels the practices in the Middle and Lower Yangzi valley, especially in Hunan (Allard 2018).

Recent scholarship emphasizes continuities over disruptions in the Neolithic to Bronze Age transition in the Yangzi Basin, including the local contexts, and possibly origins, of metallurgy. Still, the introduction of Central Plains-style bronze casting around 1500 BCE had a momentous effect on the southern communities and networks. The pursuit of resources, labor, and technical expertise needed for manufacturing hundred-kilogram-heavy vessels, bells, and figures strengthened exchange networks and fueled the consolidation of centralized institutions. Throughout the Yangzi valley, new mines were opened, new palaces and citadels were built, and foundries were churning out shiny bronzes flaunted in royal funeral processions and solemn shrine services.

The emergence of hereditary monarchical authority, intimated by the Dayangzhou mausoleum, and the professionalization of the ruling class, possibly reflected by the Sanxingdui images, have been interpreted as the markers of state organization (Liu and Chen 2012) and, as such, find close parallels in the contemporaneous developments on the Central Plains. At the same time, lesser stress on individual or lineage pedigree, wealth, and leadership, along with the prevalence of "communal" rituals of nature-worshipping, illustrate multiple coordination strategies forged in the course of institutional and ideological experimentation in the early Bronze Age southern East Asia.

Powering these changes was the new dynamics of intercommunal competition. The advent of the Bronze Age revolutionized warfare more than any other human activity, and the destruction of Wucheng, along with the impressive array of metal weapons in its possible ruler's tomb, is the earliest unambiguous evidence of large-scale organized intercommunal violence in the South. However, the intensity and geographical scale of this violence were considerably less than in contemporaneous north China. Unlike the Late Shang rulers, no leader of a Yangzi-based polity campaigned across hundreds of kilometers and executed prisoners of war in tens of thousands (Campbell 2014b; Campbell 2018).

During the centuries after 1000 BCE, the synergy of expanding long-distance networks and centralization of power, coupled with the sharp increase in influences and interventions from the Central Plains, thoroughly transformed the institutional landscape of southern East Asia and left a lasting footprint on its environment. These are the subjects of the next section.

5 States and Networks: Southern East Asia Meets China, 1000–250 BCE

In 1046 BCE, an alliance of bellicose clans from the western fringes of the Central Plains captured the Shang capital. Through a combination of military strategy, network-building, and institutional innovation, the coalition leaders, known as the royal house of Zhou, created a sphere of elite interaction that stretched from the Wei River Basin in the west to the Shandong Peninsula in the east and from the environs of present-day Beijing in the north to the Middle Yangzi in the south. This commonwealth of aristocratic lineages shared the rituals of ancestor worshiping, used the Chinese writing system, and recognized the authority of the Zhou kings. This created a framework for extensive cooperation: intermarriages, diplomatic communication, exchange of resources, and human mobility. Over the eight centuries surveyed in this section, this cooperation increasingly defined the Zhou sphere vis-à-vis the outsiders. Around 250 BCE, some societies in East Asia were distinctly "Chinese," while others were not (Falkenhausen 2006a; Vogt 2020).

The balance of power between these two worlds gradually shifted in favor of the former. The Western Zhou (1046–771 BCE) kings suffered severe setbacks at the hands of groups outside the Zhou sphere, some of which made deep incursions into the Central Plain and destroyed several Zhou-affiliated regional polities at the beginning of the Spring and Autumn era (771–453 BCE). However, during the Warring States period (453–221 BCE), the Sinitic states (i.e., Zhou-sphere polities, elites of which were versed in Chinese literary tradition) were on the offensive, pushing their frontiers into northern grasslands, western highlands, and subtropical hill country south of the Yangzi. They achieved this through improvements in military technology, and, more importantly, by developing new institutions of intensive cooperation: bureaucratic government, written laws, centralized taxation, and resource management. The Western Zhou pioneered some far-reaching innovations, but crucial changes took place after 600–500 BCE (Hsu 1965; Lewis 1999; Li 2008).

By 250 BCE, these new-model polities became the motors of social and environmental change, and their elites transformed the peer networks of trans-regional interaction into territorial states, where resources within more or less clearly defined borders were exploited exclusively by a single political center. Two states, Qin and Chu, scrambled to carve out the spheres of interest in southern East Asia, leading to the emergence of an empire.

5.1 The Zhou Commonwealth and the Making of the Sinitic Network

The Western Zhou was a loose confederacy of largely autonomous regional domains, some of which preexisted the Zhou conquest of Shang, while others were parceled out to the relatives, allies, and even former enemies of the Zhou kings. This network was tied together by a religious culture centered on the Zhou rulers and their ancestors and ritual-embedded redistribution of resources, particularly land, dependent laborers, and metals to cast vessels for ancestral offerings. Many of these vessels carried inscriptions – all members of the Zhou commonwealth used the Chinese writing system that fully developed during the Late Shang period – that disseminated a shared vision of kingship and elite identity. In the words of Vogt (2023: 257), the Zhou state "was bound by bronze, in that the messages carried by bronze vessels held it together."

The core groups of the Zhou coalition were organized into exogamous patrilineal lineages. The exchange of brides helped to maintain kinship connections among the Zhou elites and integrate new participants into the Zhou political sphere (Khayutina 2017; Vogt 2020). The royal house leveraged the power of ritual and writing to sustain cooperation within the commonwealth even after the coercive capacity of its monarchs shrank in the wake of military defeats and succession crises. In particular, the Zhou court stood up to the challenge of elite overproduction – the demographic expansion of aristocratic lineages that exacerbated competition over resources within the Zhou elite – by reforming the all-important system of ancestor worshipping. The ritual reform (ca. 950–850 BCE) introduced more rigorous hierarchical differentiation within the lineages and enhanced the Zhou group identity through new ceremonies that highlighted the relations between the king and the elites of the regional polities (Rawson 1999; Falkenhausen 2006a: 29–73; Vogt 2023: 176–96).

The simultaneous adoption of new ritual norms throughout the Zhou world attests to the center's ability to plan and carry out a complex reform program (Falkenhausen 2006a: 29–30). Despite the ongoing debates about the nature of the Western Zhou polity, the Zhou appear to have adopted a more systematic approach to the administration of their core regions than the preceding Shang. Equally innovative was their military organization that for the first time introduced standing royal armies. Regional polities emulated some of these institutions, planting the seeds of administrative standardization (Li 2008; Li 2013: 139–60; Vogt 2020).

Zhou's institutional ingenuity had to do with the fact that their polity-building project developed in the geographical interface between the Central Plains and the western highlands and from the beginning relied on the integration of diverse groups and regionally specific resources and skills: Shang bronze-casters, scribes, and administrators, horse-breeders from the northwestern grasslands, experts in Steppe-style hand-to-hand combat, mining communities in the Yangzi copper belt (Rawson 2015; Rawson 2017; Rawson, Huan, and Taylor 2021; Sun 2021). By inserting themselves as a passing point in multiple interaction networks, the Zhou leaders came to control the know-how and flows of resources central to the political economy of the emerging commonwealth. Recent metallographic studies of the Western

Zhou vessels and weapons suggest that the Zhou court controlled the circulation of metals used in bronze production among the regional polities (Li et al. 2020; Hsu et al. 2021). The Zhou monarchs might have also centralized redistribution of other items of elite consumption, including high-quality ritual vessels cast by the royal foundries and high-fired stoneware from the kilns in the Lower Yangzi. And for the first time, the geographical expansion of Central Plains political networks had a direct and transformative impact on the social, political, and economic landscapes of southern East Asia.

5.2 State Formation in the Yangzi Valley

Western Zhou was the first northern-based polity to institutionalize its presence in the Yangzi valley. Soon after the defeat of the Shang, the Zhou rulers established or accepted into the Zhou commonwealth the polity of Zeng 曾, which was located on a northern tributary of Middle Yangzi (**Figure 7**). Along with a number of smaller military garrisons, Zeng became the major conduit of Zhou cultural influence and economic interests in the south. The inscriptions on bronze vessels excavated from the tombs of Zeng leaders reflect their participation in the Zhou system of aristocratic titles, ancestral sacrifices, and inter-polity communication (Venture 2017; Fang 2018; Chen 2019).

Finds of Western Zhou bronzes in the Lake Dongting region indicate partial adoption of the Zhou ritual culture by the local elites. The Zhou expansion into

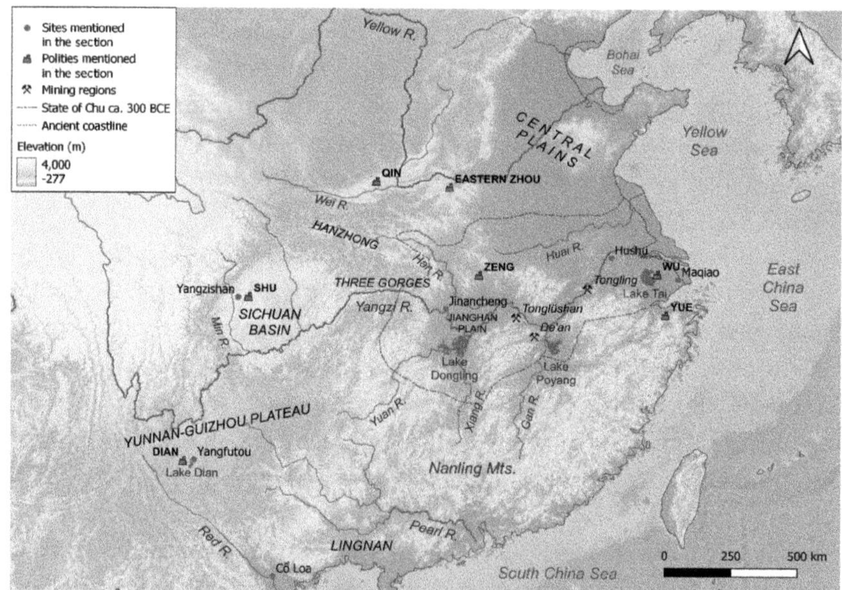

Figure 7 Southern East Asia in the first millennium BCE. Map by the author.

the region and exchanges between Zhou client polities north of the river and the local groups were probably driven by the quest for metal ores. Copper extraction at Tonglüshan increased during this period, and large indigenous settlements emerged at the edges of the eastern Hubei mining region (Hu 2015; Wu 2022). Finds of copper ingots in the elite tombs of Zeng highlight its role as a transportation hub for the Yangzi metals heading north to the Zhou foundries (Khayutina 2017; Chen 2019: 59). During the Eastern Zhou era (771–221 BCE), Zeng remained a major bronze-casting center and became a valuable ally to the new dominant power in the Yangzi valley, the state of Chu.

Despite their ongoing exchanges with the Central Plains polities, communities in the Lower Yangzi valley stayed outside the Zhou culture sphere well into the first millennium BCE. The ceramic traditions of the second-millennium BCE Hushu 湖熟 and Maqiao cultures continued uninterrupted, and new funerary forms that developed after ca. 1000 BCE, such as ground-level mounded tombs, some of which enclosed stone cists, have no parallels in the Zhou, although they may reflect northern Steppe influences (Rawson 2023: 205–30). Foundries along the Lower Yangzi used a distinctive high-tin alloy to cast weapons and tools, as well as bronze vessels modeled on the Shang-period Central Plains prototypes. Despite the imports of the Zhou vessels, including some inscribed ones, the local elites did not take notice of ritual innovations that accompanied the reorganization of the Zhou lineages after the mid-tenth century BCE (Falkenhausen 2006a: 271–84).

From the sixth century onward, growing interactions with the Zhou polities, especially the Chu on the Middle Yangzi (see Section 5.3), brought about selective adoption of the Zhou mortuary tradition – vertical pits with wooden tomb furniture, sloping entry ramps, horse-and-chariot pits, and bronze objects that likely originated in the Chu workshops – by the elites in the western part of the Lower Yangzi valley. This coincided with the rapid accession of the most powerful local polity, the Wu 吳 (with a center in the present-day Jiangsu Province), into the Zhou world, culminating in its ruler's participation in the commonwealth's covenant in 482 BCE and his claim to seniority in the royal Ji 姬 clan. According to some later texts, the rulers of Wu and its archrival Yue 越 (based in the present-day Zhejiang Province) also initiated ambitious state-building programs that involved infrastructural development, construction of capital cities, and introduction of Zhou-style government institutions: professional administrators, standing armies, and state-managed agriculture. The same texts also hint at the continuing maritime orientation of the Lower Yangzi populations, their seaborne migrations, and connections to the coastal communities south of the Yangzi Delta (Falkenhausen 2006a: 282–84; Milburn 2010: 91–121; Brindley 2015: 85–92).

Surrounded by the mountains and relatively insulated from both the Central Plains and regions downstream the Yangzi River, populations of the Sichuan Basin had far less contact with the Zhou world than the communities in the Middle and Lower Yangzi valley. Local sociopolitical dynamics remained the crucial factor in the development of centralized institutions well into the second half of the first millennium BCE, although external contacts, not necessarily with the Central Plains, played a certain role. Sometime after 1150 BCE, the population center in the western part of the basin drifted to the Chengdu area. Material-cultural continuities between Sanxingdui and Jinsha, the new central settlement located within the present-day city of Chengdu, suggest that some of the Sanxingdui elites may have relocated their polity to a new site (Flad and Chen 2013: 94–100; H. Sun 2013; Shelach-Lavi 2015: 245–46).

The finds at Jinsha reveal the growing social stratification and intra- and intercommunal conflict at the turn of the first millennium BCE, including the already-mentioned stone figures of captives or enslaved persons (Zhu, Zhang, and Wang 2006; Flad and Chen 2013: 99). A later Chinese text mentions several Sichuan groups as members of the Zhou coalition against the Shang, and archaeological finds hint at intensified contacts between the Chengdu Plain and the Wei River Basin around 1000 BCE (Sage 1992: 34–42; Falkenhausen 2011; Sun 2018). Was the steepening of social hierarchies and increase in organized coercion in the Sichuan Basin stimulated by the extension and militarization of the elite networks? If so, these contacts were not primarily oriented toward the Central Plains for the better part of the first millennium BCE. The period between 800 and 500 BCE appears to have been the time of Sichuan's relative isolation from the core regions of the Zhou commonwealth and of growing interactions with the highland people north and south of the Chengdu Plain (Falkenhausen 1996; Yao 2016: 118–21).

When written and material evidence became abundant after 500 BCE, the Chengdu Plain was under the control of the Shu 蜀 polity under the Kaiming 開明 Dynasty, the first Sichuan-based ruling house mentioned in the Chinese sources. They engaged in sporadic communication with the Zhou states, presided over large-scale construction projects, such as the ritual mound at Yangzishan 羊子山, and were capable of mustering military forces for campaigns outside the Sichuan Basin. The ubiquity of distinctive seals in elite burials on the Chengdu Plain indicates uniform practices of ownership and correspondence, possibly backed by the state. The emergence of a local script (which remains undeciphered) should have facilitated the nascent written administration (Sage 1992: 73–78; Song 2008: 219–21; Flad and Chen 2013: 101–6).

If the story of Sinitic expansion and state formation in southern East Asia between 1000 and 250 BCE has a protagonist, this is the polity of Chu. Their origins are obscure. They appear to have been a minor player in the Zhou commonwealth before the eighth century BCE. However, soon after the fall of the Western Zhou, the Chu embarked on territorial expansion from their advantageously located base in the Middle Han River valley. Some of the most spectacular successes were achieved in the South. The Chu rulers came to dominate the Middle Yangzi region, where they moved their capital in the early seventh century. During the Warring States era, the Chu borders in the south extended as far as the Nanling Mountains. By 300 BCE, Chu conquered the Yue polity in the Yangzi Delta, established strongholds in the Three Gorges, and became the first power to control more than one region of southern East Asia, as well as two of the three north–south corridors and the east–west highway of the Yangzi River (Cook and Major 1999; Yang 2003; Korolkov 2022: 44–52). There is a good reason to argue that during the late Warring States period, Chu created the first empire in southern East Asia (Yates 2013; Takamura 2019).

As in the case of the Zhou itself, the Chu success was probably defined by a felicitous combination of networking and intensive political and military coordination. The Chu-led alliance of polities on the southern fringe of the Central Plains and in the Han River valley mimicked the Zhou commonwealth. The Chu elite adopted the key Zhou institutions of kingship, lineage organization, ancestral rituals, and written communication while the Chu rulers arrogated the Zhou royal title (Falkenhausen 2003; Falkenhausen 2006a: 262–71), effectively diverting the Zhou institutional arsenal toward the Yangzi-based state-building project. Homogenization of funerary culture within the Chu domains indicates the spread of shared religious beliefs and lifestyles (Li 1991; Yang 2000: 64–145; Gao 2012; Flad and Chen 2013: 133–34), perhaps as the result of interaction at the elite level, but possibly also reflecting intensified economic and cultural connections and human migrations north and south of the Middle Yangzi. By founding their capital at the heart of Jianghan Plain, the Chu leaders tapped into the fast-developing agricultural region with enormous economic and demographic potential: a possible explanation for their ability to field huge armies throughout the Eastern Zhou era. Finally, Chu's geographical location at the intersection of the Zhou world and the non-Sinitic societies in the Yangzi valley and further south incentivized administrative and financial innovation that made Chu one of the pioneers of power centralization in East Asia.

5.3 Institutionalization of Centralized Power, ca. 600–250 BCE

The Zhou institutions that shaped the geographic outlines of the Sinitic world started to unravel long before a succession crisis and an external invasion spelled the end of the Western Zhou in 771 BCE. The Zhou rulers' capacity to centralize resources was weak, and one major defeat proved enough to fatally undermine their military power. Although Zhou's innovations in network-building helped to sustain the ritual authority of the Zhou monarchs until the fourth century BCE, crucial Zhou institutions such as diplomacy, elite intermarriage, and ritual assemblies could also be used by the client polities to create their alliances, as illustrated by the case of Chu. Political thinkers of the Eastern Zhou era rightly saw the appropriation of these institutions by the regional rulers and their power-mongering ministers as the source of violent competition among the Sinitic polities and internecine strife within many of them.

The process of political centralization in East Asia during the Eastern Zhou era is well-known in its general outlines (Hsu 1965; Lewis 1990; Kiser and Cai 2003; Lander 2021). The growing scale and organizational sophistication of warfare favored centralized planning and control of resources. Disenfranchised cadet branches of aristocratic lineages switched their allegiance to polity rulers and staffed their incipient administrations. As the population increased, farmer households settled in formerly peripheral territories and created swaths of cultivated land outside the control of lineage leaders, potentially available for unmediated taxation by the center. Agricultural expansion gained momentum during the Warring States period when the use of ox-drawn iron plows facilitated the reclamation of heavy alluvial soils in the river plains (Falkenhausen 2006a: 284–87; Liu 2017: 26–39; Korolkov and Hein 2021).

From the eighth century onward, expansive polities at the periphery of the Zhou world experimented with novel administrative forms. The Chu rulers were among the first to appoint magistrates on the conquered territories instead of delegating authority to the local potentates (Creel 1964; Li 2013: 166–67). By the Warring States period, counties (*xian* 縣) became the mainstay of centralized territorial administration. In Chu, they were complemented by hereditary rulers appointed by the king mainly from the members of the royal clan, and military commanderies along the frontiers (Zheng 2012; Chen 2018; Korolkov 2022: 49–50). This promiscuous administration reflects the guiding principle of the Chu government: maintaining the balance between, on the one hand, the need to centralize resources to ensure the polity's survival and, on the other, the interests of the powerful aristocracy (including the royal house) that was the principal stakeholder in the Chu state-building project and staffed the top echelon of its rapidly expanding bureaucracy (Chen 1996).

As elsewhere in Sinitic East Asia, population growth in the Chu territories along the Middle Yangzi provided resources and opportunities for institutional innovation. By the fourth century BCE, settlers from Chu's core region north of the river poured into Hunan, largely replacing indigenous populations around Lake Dongting. The state followed in the wake and established fortified administrative towns and customs stations along the main river valleys (Falkenhausen 2006a: 285–86; Korolkov 2022: 45–47). On the Jianghan Plain, the Chu capital Ying 郢 (the archaeological site is known as Jinancheng 紀南城), with a walled area of ca. 16 km^2, may have had several hundred thousand residents (Yang 2000: 36–45; Xu 2017: 294–96). Supplying such a city would have required remaking the plain's ecosystem to intensify land use and facilitate imports from outside the region. Written sources from the early imperial era (221 BCE–220 CE) report that the Chu built a canal between the Han River and the Yunmeng wetlands, probably to deliver grain and other products to its capital (Sima 2006: 29.1407). An excavated document from the early second century BCE testifies to the construction of flood-prevention dikes north and south of the Middle Yangzi during the Warring States period. Such projects helped to reclaim ever larger stretches of wetland in the Chu metropolitan region (Lander 2014; Lander 2022a).

Along with its expanding government and military apparatus, the Chu metropolitan center on the Jianghan Plain absorbed resources from across the Yangzi Basin and beyond. As the mutually reinforcing processes of power centralization and amassment of the population in metropolitan areas accelerated during the Warring States period, each state scrambled to lay claims on the heretofore acephalous networks of interregional exchanges. Some cities on the Central Plains were casting coins as early as the seventh century BCE, but it was the states at the periphery of the Sinitic world, such as Chu and Qin, that centralized coinage and used coined money to create closed currency zones and monopolize control of resource circulation (Peng 2000; Emura 2011; Von Glahn 2016: 60–66; Zhao et al. 2021). The Chu rulers also sought to directly administer trade by awarding some privileged agents with toll exemptions along prescribed routes between the Chu center and newly conquered territories (Chen 1989; Falkenhausen 2005). During the Warring States period, the Chu settlers, probably followed by administrators and troops, moved into the Tonglüshan copper belt and the salt-producing areas in the Three Gorges, some 400 km upstream of the Chu capital, to claim control over these crucial commodities for the state of Chu (Zhu 2010; Flad 2011: 224–27; Wu 2022).

After the sixth century BCE, institutional centralization spearheaded by the Chu spread across southern East Asia, first reaching the regions closest and best connected to the Middle Yangzi. The Wu and Yue elites in the Lower Yangzi valley adopted Zhou culture in its Chu forms (Falkenhausen 2006a: 278), and their rulers most likely relied on the Chu templates for their state-strengthening reforms. Chinese written records and, especially in the case of Wu, archaeological finds suggest that the two polities heavily invested in the construction of huge walled capitals, agricultural reclamation of deltaic wetlands, and transportation infrastructures (Feng 2007: 38–59; Milburn 2010: 91–121). When the Lower Yangzi valley became part first of the Chu at the end of the fourth century BCE and then of the Qin Empire around 220 BCE, both states used this artificial landscape to establish territorial administration and integrate the region into their polities. The spread of Chu trade networks into Lingnan and Southwestern Highlands had an equally momentous impact on the local societies and the ways they engaged with the broader world.

5.4 Polity Growth and Transregional Networks in Lingnan and Southwestern Highlands

Musing on the origins of the political order in the Southwestern Highlands, the great Han historian Sima Qian 司馬遷 (ca. 145–86 BCE) narrates about the Chu general Zhuang Qiao 莊蹻 who, in the late fourth century BCE, conquered the alluvial plain around Lake Dian in central Yunnan and established the Dian royal dynasty (Sima 2006: 116.2993). In the centuries to follow, Chinese historiography produced numerous accounts about Sinitic individuals – princes, courtiers, and military commanders – who established states among the indigenous populations at the edges of the Zhou world. Modern scholars are no longer taking these stories at their face value. Recent archaeological excavations documented the gradual centralization of wealth, military power, and technical expertise in various parts of southern East Asia during the first millennium BCE leading to the formation of regional polities, such as the Dian in the Central Lakes Basin of Yunnan, Cổ Loa (sometimes associated with the Âu Lạc kingdom of the later Chinese and Vietnamese written tradition) in the Red River Delta, and the Yue groups in Guangdong and Guangxi (Allard 1997; Kim 2015; Yao 2016).

Some factors behind this development were distinctly local. The sea level decline between 2000 and 1 BCE, which ranged between 0.5 m and 4 m along the coast of the South China Sea, accelerated the formation of the Red and Pearl River Deltas (Tanabe et al. 2003; Weng 2007; Li 2015). Their fertile alluvial soils were gradually reclaimed by rice farmers who advanced from the hillsides flanking the river valleys and benefited from the introduction of metal plowshares to turn over heavy alluvium. A total of ninety-six bronze plowshares have been recovered from a single bronze drum excavated at Cổ Loa, a heavily fortified settlement in the Lower Red River valley. At the peak of its extant, Cổ Loa's walls, the construction of which started in the fourth century BCE, enclosed an area of approximately 600 ha. Kim (2015: 203) contends that "the sustained, organized, and directed construction effort necessary to result in Cổ Loa's monumental system of ramparts would have required a durable and bureaucratic political system" and other "institutional trappings of a state."

The large volume of crossbow arrowheads stockpiled at the Cổ Loa citadel, and the prevalence of weapons in contemporaneous Dong Son Culture burials in the Lower Red River valley suggest that coercion played a crucial role in the emergence of this polity and that contacts increased with the Sinitic world, where the crossbow technology developed during the Warring States period (Higham 2014: 203–11; Kim 2015: 236–37). The two processes were probably interrelated. In the lake basins of central Yunnan, too, agricultural intensification that involved the spread of multi-cropping and plowing (Dal Martello 2020; Dal Martello, Li, and Fuller 2021) caused not only population growth, expansion of settlement, intercommunal coordination, and consolidation of social elites but also an upsurge in violence, as "the taking of captives and headhunting become political themes that are depicted with increasing frequency and realism" (Yao 2016: 174). This was the background for the formation, after ca. 500 BCE, of the Dian polity, the leaders of which controlled the regional exchange networks for prestige goods, accumulated wealth on a scale unparalleled in the surrounding highlands, and monopolized the regalia of power, such as the bronze drums used in military rituals (Churchman 2015; Yao 2016: 131–63).

Just as the power of the Dian rested on the growing agricultural and demographic resources of the Yunnan lacustrine basins, it was also embedded in their position at the node of preexisting and emerging long-distance exchanges. Interactions along the western corridor, which connected the highlands to the Sichuan Basin and Eurasian grasslands in the north, intensified during the first millennium BCE. After 500 BCE, Chu influences and imports, including crossbows and other weapons, became increasingly visible in the mortuary culture of the Dian elites, indicating the expansion of the Chu trade networks into the Southwestern Highlands (Falkenhausen 1996; Chiou-Peng 1998; Murowchick 2001; Yao 2016: 141–48). Yunnan mines had long been supplying metals, especially tin and lead, to the bronze foundries in the Yangzi and Yellow River valleys, and in the latter half of the first millennium BCE, the highlands emerged as one of the leading providers of horses and slaves – another token of escalating intercommunal conflict – to the markets in the north. The burgeoning transregional horse trade provides a context for the arrival of people with possibly steppe connections to the Southwestern Highlands after 400 BCE (Zhang et al. 2018).

While there is little evidence of polity formation in northern Lingnan before the Qin conquest in 214 BCE (see Section 6), the social landscape of Guangdong and Guangxi was destabilized by the growing contacts with the Yangzi valley, which created opportunities for self-aggrandizing individuals to exploit their privileged access to prestige goods networks. After ca. 600 BCE, Chu-style bronze vessels, bells, and weapons proliferated in the wealthy tombs that concentrated along the rivers leading to the Nanling passes (Allard 1997; Falkenhausen 2002; Allard 2017). The appearance of the so-called Yue-style bronzes and "narrow graves" in Lingnan after 500 BCE possibly indicates the migration of indigenous populations from the Middle and Lower Yangzi valley under the pressure of Chu expansion, which culminated in the destruction of the Yue polity around 330 BCE. Just as in Yunnan and the Red River Delta, integration in more extensive exchange networks was accompanied by mounting violence, probably ignited by the conflicts over the control of trade resources and routes. Weapons, especially pikes and swords, became so widespread in Lingnan by the late Warring States era that specimens were excavated from almost every tomb that contained bronze (Müller 2004; Huang 2015: 285–86).

A bronze drum excavated from an elite tomb at Yangfutou 羊甫頭 north of Lake Dian, probably dated to the fifth century BCE, bears an image of a boat rowed by plumed warriors (**Figure 8**). After 500 BCE, these bronze drums, and the iconographic motif of rowing warriors, became extremely popular among the elites in the Lower Red River valley and, somewhat later, in Guangxi and Guangdong (Prüch 1999: 152–55; Kim 2015: 137–41; Yao 2016: 138). Bellicose leaders of political-military networks in the Southwestern Highlands and Lingnan consolidated their authority by extending frontiers of trading and raiding. By the time the Qin and Han imperial armies marched south in the late third and second centuries BCE, they followed in the tracks of generations of indigenous warriors, merchants, and explorers who rowed their boats up and down the Red and Pearl Rivers and the South China Sea coast in search of wealth and political allies.

By 250 BCE, Sinitic states became a powerful factor in the lives of people throughout southern East Asia. Populations of the Yangzi valley found themselves paying tributes and taxes, supplying military recruits, and abiding by the laws of the up-and-coming powers of Qin and Chu. South of the great river, the expansion of exchange networks and population movements set in motion by the Qin and Chu conquests in the Yangzi Basin had a profoundly destabilizing

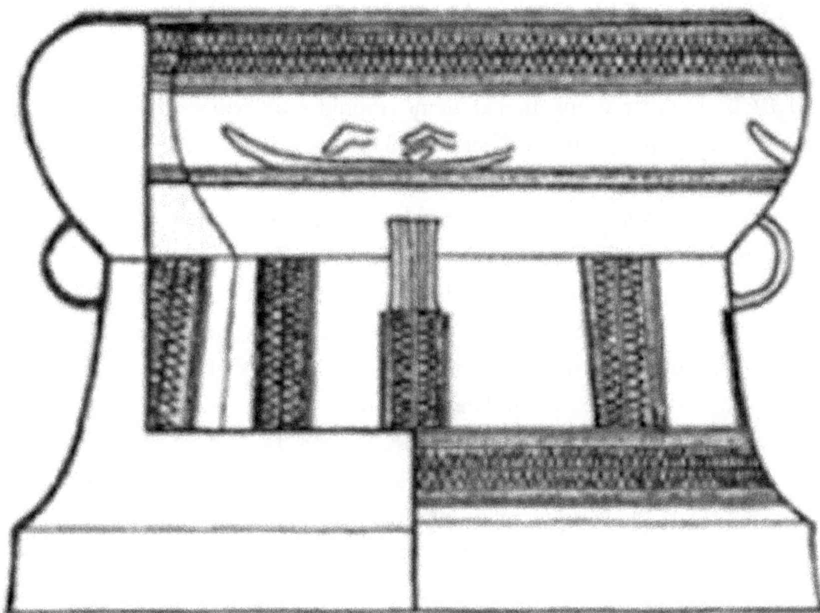

Figure 8 Rowing warriors on a bronze drum from Yangfutou, Yunnan, ca. fifth century BCE. Source: Yao, A. (2016). *The Ancient Highlands of Southwest China. From the Bronze Age to the Han Empire.* Oxford: Oxford University Press.

impact, accelerating elite formation, intercommunal violence, and consolidation of political authority within the local societies.

Environmental historian Robert Marks (2012: 58) observed that the "combination of a central state with farming families linked by markets proved to be a distinctively Chinese way of organizing their society, and of transforming nature." States and markets – the paradigmatic institutions of intensive and extensive cooperation discussed in Section 1 – developed during the Eastern Zhou era and have since served as the principal motors of spatial expansion of the Sinitic world. This section traced the mutually reinforcing development of centralized and decentralized institutions, which eventually allowed the Central Plains-based polities to tie the rest of East Asia into their network, back to the beginnings of the Western Zhou commonwealth around 1000 BCE.

While the Western Zhou laid the foundation for transregional coordination of political, economic, and cultural behaviors among the aristocratic lineages, the Eastern Zhou institutional change enabled – and often enforced – participation of broader social strata across a wider geographical sphere in the Sinitic polities and networks. The power of the state and the power of markets fueled the Sinitic conquest of southern East Asia which gained momentum in the third century BCE.

6 Southern East Asia in the Sinitic Empire, 250 BCE–300 CE

As favorable climate conditions known as the Classical Optimum set in around 250 BCE, bumper crops fueled demographic expansion in the Old World civilizational cores (Zou and Zhang 2013; Brooke 2014). Vast regions of Italy and the central Mediterranean were settled on a massive scale (Terrenato 2007). A regional survey of ancient settlement sites in eastern China revealed a demographic explosion between the Eastern Zhou and the Han periods (Feinman, Nicholas, and Hui 2010). Overall, China's population increased from an estimated twenty million at the end of the third century BCE to sixty million by the turn of the common era (Ge 2000: 300–12; Shang 2003). As a result, states in the west and east of Eurasia did not lack soldiers to fight the wars that, during the third and second centuries BCE, forged the two most powerful and expansive polities of global antiquity: the Roman Republic (later the Empire) and the early Chinese empires of Qin and Han.

These empires were, first and foremost, the powerful states that surpassed their peers in mobilizing manpower and resources, providing centralized command, and creating strong group identities to ensure high levels of commitment by their fighting men. This was achieved through a variety of institutional arrangements, from inclusive forms of civic community, in the case of the Roman Republic, to radical meritocracy and pervasive bureaucratic administration, in the case of Qin and Han (Mann 1986; Lewis 2007; Taylor 2020).

But these formidable states did not expand into the vacuum. Their armies, diplomats, and colonists followed preexisting connectivity routes and redirected the flows of wealth and labor toward the imperial rulers and their allies in the newly acquired provinces. Larger populations, more productive farming, and denser trade networks favored empire-builders not only because more spear-won booty could be appropriated immediately after the conquest but also by creating opportunities for the economies of scale, which disproportionately accrued to the local power holders. More extensive markets and greater concentration of consumer power, prominently represented by the imperial capitals and armies, allowed landed and mercantile elites to capitalize on their wealth while trading leverage in their communities for the imperial support of local hierarchies (Bang 2008; Bang 2012).

As the empires were negotiated between the central rulers and their provincial collaborators, they were increasingly held together not by force and centralized administration but by the economic, cultural, and political networks of their elites within vaguely defined geographical zones (Crooks and Parsons 2016; Crossley 2016; Haldon 2021). Correspondingly, following the initial conquest, the impact of the empires was exerted not so much through violence (although its threat never subsided) as through the institutions of extensive cooperation: value equivalencies, uniform coinage, maintenance of property rights, literacy (Morris 2014; Terpstra 2019). By the same token, although the empires could transform the environment through extraordinary concentration of coercion – reconfiguring natural hydraulic systems in massive labor projects, reducing thriving cities to desert, or, conversely, transforming arid grasslands into agricultural frontiers through forced resettlement of farmer colonists – it was their capacity to perpetuate and expand "business as usual" that left behind the extensive traces of anthropogenic pollution during the period of peace, prosperity, and hands-off policies in the ancient Eurasian empires during the first two centuries CE (Brooke 2014).

Ancient empires are an appropriate subject for the final section of this Element. They bundled together the two types of institutions, "states" and "networks," with such efficiency and on such a scale as to set in motion the sustained expansion of the Old World economic and cultural interactions known as the late antique and medieval globalizations (Abu-Lughod 1989; Preiser-Kapeller 2018; Hermans 2020).

6.1 Early Sinitic Empires in Southern East Asia

In the late fourth century BCE, it looked like the state of Chu was on the track to unify southern East Asia (see Section 5). But around the middle of the same century, a series of state-strengthening reforms transformed the northwestern polity of Qin into a formidable military power. The population of the Qin homeland in the Wei River valley had long-established connections with Hanzhong and Sichuan in the Yangzi Basin. In 316 BCE, Qin annexed the Chengdu Plain, and in 280–278 BCE conquered the Chu capital on the Middle Yangzi. In a series of blitzkrieg campaigns between 230 and 221 BCE, the Qin armies subjugated the entire Zhou ecumene. The king of Qin proclaimed himself the First August Thearch. In English, this title is conventionally rendered as "emperor," making the Qin the first in a 2,000-year-long line of Chinese empires.

In the south, Qin took over the Chu sphere in the Lower and Middle Yangzi but did not stop there. In 214 BCE, the emperor ordered his troops to cross the Nanling Mountains. Overcoming fierce local resistance, they established three commanderies along the Pearl River and at the eastern fringe of the Yunnan-Guizhou Plateau. For the first time, the populations of Lingnan and Southwestern Highlands fell under the direct control of a Sinitic state.

Qin's military success was backed by the highly centralized bureaucratic apparatus that managed people and resources across the vast realm. This hyper-centralization backfired as the government's capacity to control its agents spread thin, the costs of the command economy skyrocketed, and functionaries in provinces lacked commitment to the system that subjected them to relentless monitoring (Korolkov 2021). The Qin Empire barely outlived its founder and collapsed amid a massive rebellion headed by the surviving members of old Warring States aristocracies and disaffected imperial officials.

The power vacuum that the Qin left behind in southern East Asia was filled by multiple regional polities that amalgamized Qin institutions with local political traditions. Some of them, such as the princedom of Changsha 長沙 south of the Middle Yangzi, owed formal allegiance to the Han Empire, which consolidated control over the core Qin territories after 202 BCE. Others, such as Nanyue 南越 (203–111 BCE) in Lingnan, were independent states often in conflict with the Han (**Figure 9**). Regardless of their relationships with the new Sinitic Empire in the north, these polities relied on the Qin institutional legacy – unified coinage, taxation system, state organization of industries – and perpetuated circulation networks established under the Qin rule, such as the state-controlled markets for iron implements and horses (Korolkov 2022: 172–80).

The state of Nanyue illustrates these dynamics. While its rulers openly challenged the Han claims to sovereignty in the East Asian ecumene, numerous

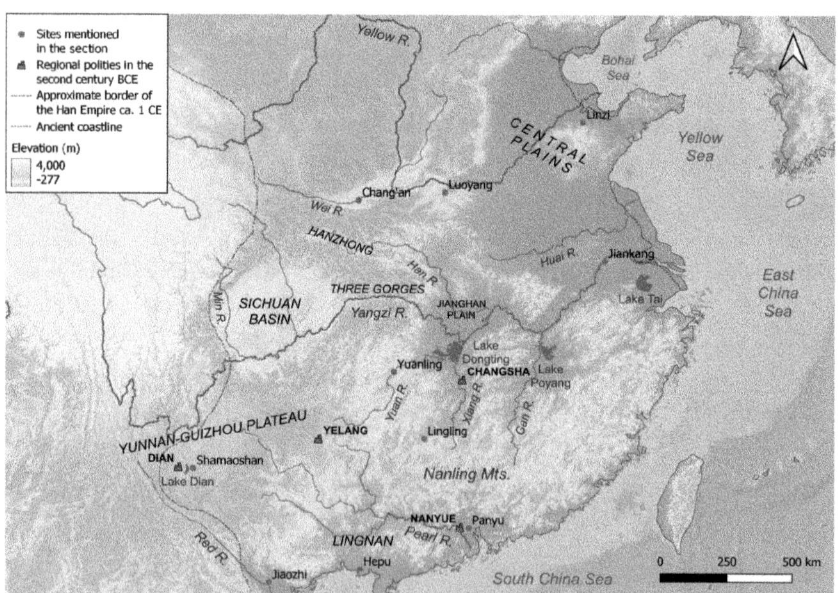

Figure 9 Southern East Asia in the age of ancient empire, 250 BCE–200 CE. Map by the author.

northern-style burials around the Nanyue capital Panyu 番禺 (present-day Guangzhou), and official documents excavated from the remains of the royal palace, indicate the presence of a considerable Sinitic diaspora and the adoption of Qin-style administrative system (Guangzhou shi wenwu kaogu yanjiusuo et al. 2022). Bronze coins appeared in Lingnan during the Qin period, and the use of imperial coinage became widespread under the Nanyue. This facilitated participation in cross-regional trade, particularly the imports of iron tools from the north. The use of iron spread in Lingnan from the late third century BCE, probably in conjunction with the official promulgation of iron metallurgy by the Qin. The founding ruler of Nanyue, Zhao Tuo 趙佗 (r. 203–137 BCE), went to war when the Han court tried to suspend iron trade across the Nanling Mountains, a token of the region's growing dependence on the imperial technologies and markets (Sima 2006: 113.2969; Lam et al. 2020; Korolkov 2022: 176).

When the reinvigorated Han Empire set out on territorial expansion in the middle of the second century BCE, they faced an institutional landscape markedly different from the one the Qin had to deal with some seventy years earlier. From the perspective of the imperial government in Chang'an, this landscape became more continuous and legible. Sino-indigenous hybrid polities, such as Changsha and Nanyue, laid the groundwork for integration into the empire. A collection of official documents from the tomb of the Marquis of Yuanling 沅陵 (d. 162 BCE) and an official archive excavated at Zoumalou 走馬樓 Street (in the present-day city of Changsha), both from the territory of the Changsha Princedom, reveal the operations of a county government in every detail identical to the Han standard (Korolkov 2022: 180–81). The Changsha rulers also carried out a thorough mapping of their domain (Ge 2004: 47–55; He 2004).

Just as the Qin and Han Empires, Changsha, Nanyue, and other southern East Asian polities in the third and second centuries BCE anchored their control to the urban centers, such as Panyu and Cổ Loa. These concentrations of population, wealth, and administrative information were taken over by the Han Empire when its armies and officials arrived on the Middle and Lower Yangzi after the suppression of a major rebellion of the regional princedoms in 154 BCE, and in Lingnan after its conquest by the Han in 111 BCE.

In the Southwestern Highlands, the Han Empire inserted itself into the local trade networks and tribal alliances. According to a transmitted account, preparations for Emperor Wu's 武帝 (141–87 BCE) campaign against Nanyue started with a diplomatic mission to ensure that Nanyue's highland partners reoriented themselves toward imperial markets that better satisfied their demand for silks (Ban 2002: 95.3839–40; Sima 2006: 116.2993–95). The Han also secured access to the Yelang 夜郎 militias that played a role in the Han conquest of

Nanyue. The ability to tap into the local military resources in the tribal zones was crucial to the maintenance of the empire, especially in southern East Asia where rough landscapes and tropical diseases limited the efficiency of imperial troops. In the highlands, the Han authorities relied on their tribal allies to quell uprisings and routinely pitted indigenous groups against each other. Similarly, a county archive recently excavated south of the Yangzi Delta indicates that the imperial navy, which was central to the Han expansion on the Pacific seaboard from the Korean Peninsula in the north to Vietnam in the south, depended on the recruitment of the local "Yue" and "Chu" marines (Cao 2022: 373).

6.2 Imperial Network

The early Chinese empires transformed preexisting interaction networks by applying the coercive power of the state, but they also had to ensure the cooperation of power holders in provinces and, as a minimum, reduce the resistance – or, better even, induce participation – of the general populace. How much of the "benefits of the empire" trickled down to ordinary households is a debated issue in the history of empires (Scheidel 2009; White 2011; Brooke 2014). The evidence from southern East Asia offers a rather optimistic picture, at least for certain areas.

To benefit their stakeholders, empires intensified resource exploitation and transfers. Human labor was the most fundamental of these resources, and the Qin and Han rulers presided over some of the largest state-organized resettlement projects in premodern history (Barbieri-Low 2021; Korolkov and Hein 2021). These relocations primarily targeted the state spaces: imperial capital, administrative towns, and their agricultural hinterlands. The Han era was a time of rapid urbanization across southern East Asia. For example, two urban belts developed along the north–south corridor between the Middle Yangzi and the Pearl River valley, which formed the backbone of imperial logistics in the region (Chen 2016: 124–29; Korolkov 2022: 190).

While the state enforced some of the migrations, they were mostly induced by the state policies, rather than organized directly. Archaeologist Liu Rui (2019: 380–89) argued that the Han conquest of Nanyue was accompanied not only by the partial destruction of its capital Panyu but also by the state investment in iron production outside the Panyu area, which resulted in temporal stagnation of agricultural development and outmigration from the former Nanyue center during the late Western Han. According to Liu, this might have been a deliberate measure to prevent the revival of the Nanyue power. Some Nanyue populations moved north of the Nanling Mountains, while others may have migrated into Yunnan (Erickson, Yi, and Nylan 2010; R. Liu 2019: 386–88).

One of the empire's principal contributions to interregional connectivity was infrastructure building. The Qin Empire opened up the Ling Canal across the Yangzi–Pearl River divide and integrated the late Warring States web of natural and artificial waterways in the Middle Yangzi, Han, and Huai River valleys into a continuous water transportation corridor. It made possible the shipment of southern grain to the imperial storehouses near Luoyang 洛陽, which were used to supply the Qin and Han capitals further west (Xin 2013). As the government of the Eastern Han Empire (25–220 CE) scrambled to consolidate its control of Lingnan in the wake of a major rebellion in 40–43 CE, it organized the construction of a trunk road across the Nanling Mountains, which complemented the water route (Korolkov 2022: 185–86).

The spread of iron metallurgy in southern East Asia is an example of the link between imperial expansion and technological diffusion that affected the lives of ordinary households. East Asian populations had been familiar with bloomery smelting (early form of iron smelting that produced a porous mass of iron and slag) since the eighth century BCE, if not earlier, but by the fifth century BCE, metallurgists in the Central Plains pioneered the cast iron technology that used larger blast furnaces and created conditions for scaling up production, conditioned on the availability of vast amounts of ore and fuel and sophisticated labor organization (Needham and Wagner 2008; Lam 2020; Lam 2023). The state was ideally positioned to provide these. Early Chinese empires were the driving force behind the spread of iron metallurgy, culminating in the foundation of the official iron monopoly under Emperor Wu, who also presided over the Han conquest of southern East Asia.

The official histories of the Han Empire mention that imperial governors in Lingnan founded state-managed ironworks to cast agricultural tools that were distributed among the local farmers. The earliest finds of iron plowshares in the region date to the Eastern Han period, when the clay models of fields worked by plow-drawing ox-teams also appeared in the local tombs. To the ancient and early medieval Chinese authors, providing access to more advanced farming tools was how the empire "benefited the people" (*li min* 利民). The sharp growth of the registered population around the Han administrative towns south of the Yangzi, which served as production and distribution centers for iron implements, suggests this was not mere rhetoric (R. Liu 2019: 66–78; Korolkov 2022: 183–91).

The middling and well-to-do urbanites reaped much of the empire's benefits. Imperial investment in infrastructure, security, and technology transfers facilitated trade and extended the range of consumption items (Barbieri-Low 2007; Sun 2008; Zhao 2014). The Qin and Han expansion contributed to monetization and growing levels of literacy underlying the commercial boom of the early imperial era. The authorities initially promulgated coinage to improve the efficiency of tax collection and state procurement. As the government came to rely on markets for a substantial part of its revenue from the mid-Western Han times onward, lubricating commerce with uniform, credible currency became an objective in itself (Von Glahn 2016: 113–20; Korolkov 2021). The progress of monetization was particularly salient in southern East Asia, where few bronze coins circulated prior to the imperial era. According to one estimate for the Guangxi Zhuang Autonomous Region, the proportion of tombs that yielded coins increased from 26 percent in the Western Han to 38 percent in the Eastern Han. Twenty-nine *banliang* coins (Qin and early Western Han) discovered in four tombs at a Western Han-period cemetery in western Hunan contrast with 4,555 *wuzhu* coins (that were cast after mid-Western Han) from sixty-six tombs at the same cemetery (Hunan sheng wenwu kaogu yanjiusuo 2006: 508–11; Korolkov 2023b).

The imperial bureaucracy, including its military branch, spearheaded the geographical expansion of Sinitic writing (Sanft 2019). Officials, with their higher-than-average level of literacy, understanding of the legal system and government institutions, and access to state infrastructure of communication, were well-positioned to participate in commerce. The figure of the official-entrepreneur is ubiquitous in the Qin and Han collections of documents excavated in the Yangzi Basin (Korolkov 2023a). From the government offices, the use of writing in economic transactions spilled over into the private sphere, leaving behind partnership agreements, business correspondence, and court records dealing with commercial disputes.

6.3 Modified Environments

The official history of the Eastern Han Empire describes one of the earliest cases of regional economic specialization in southern East Asia. In the first century CE, people of the Hepu Commandery 合浦郡 on the coast of the South China Sea in present-day Guangxi devoted themselves to pearl-hunting. They traded pearls for grain from Jiaozhi Commandery 交趾郡 in the Pearl River Delta, which at that time was going through rapid economic growth. As a result, Jiaozhi became the principal hub of the pearl trade in the Han Far South. Before too long, Hepu overharvested the pearl-bearing mollusks in its coastal waters, the quality of its pearls declined, and trade routes shifted away. The local population, which came to depend on food imports, faced starvation, and was only saved by the newly appointed Han governor, who revived local farming (Fan 1965: 76.2473).

Recent archaeological excavations at Hepu added another angle to this story. The decades around the turn of the common era were a period of particular prosperity in this area, most likely related to trade (Allard 2022). The cities of coastal Lingnan, such as Jiaozhi and Panyu, exported pearls and other wildlife products of the Far South as far as the imperial capital Chang'an 長安. Other southern regions also came to be associated with distinctive trade commodities: horses, yaks, and slaves of the Southwestern Highlands, and salt and copper of the Lower Yangzi (Sima 2006: 129.3253–83).

Yet, as far as the available evidence goes, market-driven specialization and concomitant ecological deterioration, as in the case of Hepu, were an exception rather than a rule. In the early Chinese empires, typical resource circuits were more localized than the empire-wide networks for pearls and other luxury goods, largely due to the high transportation costs. Instead, administrative urbanization, taxation, intensified land use, and population mobility created new pressures on local environments throughout East Asia.

In the Southwestern Highlands, the early stage of the Han occupation left the local political landscape largely undisturbed. Isotope analysis of human remains from Shamaoshan 紗帽山 cemetery in the Lake Dian Basin suggests the arrival of "foreigners" in the wake of the Han conquest. Most of them probably came from other southern regions – Sichuan, Lingnan, and Middle Yangzi – rather than from the Central Plains in the north. These people were integrated into local communities and buried their dead according to the local customs (Wu et al. 2019). However, sometime in the first century BCE, the settler diaspora appears to have obtained a critical mass, leading to serious changes. The population center shifted to the newly founded capital of the Han Yizhou Commandery 益州郡 with an area of 63 ha, two times larger than the largest Bronze Age settlement in the region (**Figure 10**). This was an administrative town built according to the canons of Han urban architecture. According to Yao and Jiang (2012), concentrating population in this new center was possibly "guided by imperial concerns over security and defense or an interest in expanding the availability of cultivable land on the basin floor through draining the wetlands." The archaeologically documented increase in erosion and the shift in vegetation cover point to land clearance, deforestation, and intensified paddy rice cultivation (Yao 2016: 190).

On the southern flank of the empire, the Red River Delta with its Bronze Age center at Cổ Loa remained the most densely populated imperial province south of the Yangzi throughout the Han era. Here, too, immigration picked up around the turn of the common era, particularly during the troubled reign of the usurper Wang Mang 王莽 (9–23 CE) (Fan 1965: 86.2836; Taylor 1983: 41). After crushing the massive rebellion of 40–43 CE, the Han authorities set out on

Figure 10 Excavations at Hebosuo, the capital of the Han Yizhou Commandery. **Source**: Baidu Baike.

reconstructing the local society by bringing in more immigrants, suppressing the use of bronze drums by the Dong Son aristocracy, and propagating Sinitic customs. Their effort was reinforced by the declining sea levels and deltaic plain formation, which prompted population movement from the former centers, including Cổ Loa, to the virgin alluvial soils of the eastern delta. The Han governors spearheaded land reclamation by distributing iron agricultural tools and instructing locals in advanced farming methods. By the end of the Eastern Han, the settlement landscape of the Lower Red River valley was transformed through imperial interventions combined with natural processes (Li 2015; Wei 2017; Korolkov 2023b).

Throughout southern East Asia, people were living in larger and denser communities that circulated greater numbers of goods and people across longer distances, partly in response to the empire's demand for materials and manpower. Based on the official records, between 2 and 156 CE the population of provinces along the Yangzi River and further south increased by 61 percent, or possibly as much as 72 percent, and reached sixteen million people. These numbers apply to the registered people who lived in and around the administrative towns, paid taxes, and provided labor services to the authorities. In some areas, the growth was far more abrupt. The registered population of Lingling Commandery 零陵郡 in southwestern Hunan may have increased twenty-three-fold over the last 170 years BCE, and by a further 619 percent in the first century-and-a-half of the CE (Korolkov 2022: 108).

Li et al. (2019) pointed out that the co-occurrence of rapid urbanization, rising population densities, and concomitant migrations might have been behind the possible outbreak of the tuberculosis epidemic in East Asia during the Han era, which is attested in the Middle Yangzi, among other locations. The Han chronicles report an unknown tropical disease among the Han expeditionary force on the campaign against the Nanyue in 180s BCE and, again, in the first century CE among the Han troops in Lingnan (Fan 1965: 24.840; Zhang 1998: 27–28; Sima 2006: 113.2969). These were the harbingers of catastrophic plagues that were introduced through trans-continental routes and decimated the empire's population after the 150s CE, possibly contributing to the breakdown of the ancient imperial systems across Eurasia (McNeill 1976; Brooke 2014; Preiser-Kapeller 2018).

6.4 Expansion of Nonimperial Interactions

Around the middle of the first century CE, Panyu, Hepu, and other ports on the northern coast of the South China Sea looked like typical Han towns. Government offices and private courtyard residences with tiled roofs lined the rectangular grid of streets. In their everyday lives, wealthy urbanites used exquisite lacquerware, high-fired glazed ceramics, and a variety of metropolitan-style furniture and clothing, just as their peers in Chang'an, Luoyang, or Linzi 臨淄. When they died, they were buried in brick chamber tombs that became popular empire-wide during the later Western Han era (Korolkov 2022: 191).

Yet, a visitor from the Central Plains would soon have discovered more idiosyncratic facets of urban life in the Far South. For example, the locals developed a serious passion for stone, glass, and gold bead ornaments produced with an array of drilling, soldering, granulation, and wire-making techniques with close parallels in coastal Southeast and South Asia. Some of these objects draw inspiration and technology from as far away as the Graeco-Bactrian lands in present-day Pakistan and Afghanistan (Demandt 2015). Archaeologist Bérénice Bellina (2014), who excavated an important bead-manufacturing center at the Kra Isthmus in southern Thailand, points out that among the seafaring communities of the South China Sea, these ornaments served as a form of "political currency used for legitimization, alliance-construction strategies and stabilization of authority." Their circulation created a context for craftsman migrations, the spread of specialized knowledge, and the exploitation of stone and metal deposits from Taiwan and the Philippines to Cambodia and Thailand. Our hypothetical northern visitor would have also been impressed by the ubiquity of incense burning among the coastal southerners (Li 2010). In the North, censers were luxury items reserved for crème de la crème of the imperial elite, but in Panyu, they occur in more than half of all tombs dated to the early Eastern Han, suggesting the rising imports of fragrant substances through the same trading networks that provided many of the much-coveted beads.

Neither of these consumption patterns nor their underlying production and exchange systems appear to have made substantial inroads into the empire beyond its southern maritime portals, which were partaking in two discrete circulation spheres – the East Asian imperial network and the multicenter trading world of the South Seas – but did not tie them together (Korolkov 2023b). At the same time, it was the empire-driven concentration of people and wealth in places like Panyu, Hepu, and Jiaozhi that endowed these centers with resources for interactions outside the empire.

Churchman (2016) outlines a comparable pattern in the "Land between the Two Rivers," the hilly country west of the Pearl River Delta and north of Hanoi. As the Han administrative towns thrived, and their resource-supplying networks expanded, the tribal upland groups became important economic players. Along with the forest products, their region was a key source of gold and silver, which came to be used as currencies when the supply of Han coinage started to drain out at the end of the second century CE. The strong demand for highland goods fueled competition between the local chieftains over territory and manpower needed to exploit resources, accelerating social stratification and polity formation. As the "southern empires" – the regimes with a claim to the Han legacy that formed in southern East Asia after the end of the Han Empire in 220 CE – struggled to reproduce the imperial administrative machine, highland confederacies posed a serious threat to Sinitic military and economic control in the South, not least by participating in alternative systems of value and resource circulation. An imperial edict of 375 CE complained that the "Yue people of Guangdong" melted imperial coins to cast large drums, threatening to eliminate the official currency in the region. This is a reference to the archaeologically attested revival of the so-called Bronze Drum Culture, which the Han authorities had previously repressed in its long-time center in the Red River Delta. It was duly seen as a potent framework for identity construction, manpower mobilization, and long-distance material exchanges that the empire did not control (Churchman 2016; Korolkov 2022).

The South Seas trading world and the hinterland tribal confederacies such as that in the "Land between the Rivers" were not created by the Chinese empires, but the imperial state-building and networking stimulated their consolidation and expansion. Nonimperial interactions offered their participants an opportunity to capitalize on the empire's resources while escaping its miseries: burdens of taxation and compulsory labor, social regimentation, and humiliation of having your bronze drums taken away and recast into the images of horses (Fan 1965: 24.840) – a paramount symbol of the crushing military might of distant northern overlords.

The architects of ancient East Asian empires carried out their projects in the world living through a connectivity revolution: spread of literacy and coinage, infrastructural improvements, uniformization of elite education, discourses, and tastes for material goods. Empires rarely instituted brand-new ways of extensive cooperation, but they unleashed the potential of the existing ones to intensify production and expand resource circulation for the benefit of their constituent elites. Some of the material gains trickled down to the wider masses of subjects. Those lucky enough to live in important hubs of the imperial network, such as provincial capitals and trade emporia, could enjoy a steadier food supply and a broader range of consumer goods, thanks to market integration, technology transfers, and, in the case of early Chinese empires, a state organization of new industries.

But the empire-sponsored trans-local networks and concentrations of wealth could also be used in subversive ways, to create new interaction circuits and identities that transcended and challenged imperial power. Such nonimperial networks helped to coalesce the coastal and hinterland communities along the South China Sea littoral in the early centuries CE to form a new transregional economy that spanned the Asian coastal seas and became the driver of medieval Afro-Eurasian "globalization" (Abu-Lughod 1989; Preiser-Kapeller 2018). New ideologies also rode the wave of imperial and interimperial connectivity, as famously observed by Origen (ca. 184–253) for the early Christian communities in the Roman Empire (Simić 2018). Maritime exchanges of the South China Sea facilitated the spread of Buddhism, a religion strongly associated with urban mercantile groups (Gernet 1995: 153–86; Zürcher 2013). And unseen to their human hosts, microorganisms traveled with empires' armies, merchants, and settlers to merge the previously separated disease pools into the old-world epidemiological network (McNeil 1976).

The expansion of nonimperial and trans-imperial networks destabilized ancient empires and precipitated the disintegration of their centralized institutions. Outbreaks of pandemics, mass religious movements, tribal revolts, and the elite's withdrawal from cooperation with the imperial center accompanied the decline of the Han Empire from the late second century CE. For most of the three-and-a-half centuries after the official demise of the Han in 220 CE, East Asia was divided into multiple regimes. From their new capital Jiankang 建康 (present-day Nanjing) on the southern bank of Lower Yangzi, a series of dynasties claimed sovereignty over the former Han possessions in southern East Asia, but they failed to reproduce the Han state institutions, such as household registration, capitation and agricultural taxes, official monopolies, universal military service, and policing of the countryside (S. Liu 2019; Chittick 2020).

With government revenues based on the taxation of private commerce, including long-distance maritime trade, and state administration relying on personal clientele networks, southern empires were in effect archipelagoes of commercial towns, economically vibrant, weakly centralized, and surrounded by a largely autonomous tribal hinterland and agricultural countryside controlled by the landed magnates. As such, these polities blended into the world of sea-based trading city-states of the South China Sea Basin, with whom southern courts maintained active diplomatic and cultural contacts under the peer-polity framework. Chittick (2020: 206–7) concludes that, far from being a weaker successor to the Qin and Han Empires, the "Jiankang Empire" belonged to the Sino-Southeast Asian zone, which, between the third and late sixth century CE, embarked on a trajectory leading away, not back to the "classical" model of Chinese imperial state. Its new institutional configuration included weak, unstable states and multiple overlapping, decentralized interaction networks: a remarkable resurgence of southern East Asian normality during much of the period considered in this Element.

7 Conclusion

Scholar-officials of the ancient and medieval Chinese empires and present-day anthropologists alike tend to see southern East Asia as a stateless zone, an abode of tribal groups interconnected with each other, sometimes over considerable distances, yet resistant to centralized forms of integration (Scott 2009). Accordingly, the narratives of state formation in China overwhelmingly focus on the Central Plains (Liu and Chen 2003; Liu 2004; Li 2013; Campbell et al. 2022). The Late Neolithic cultures of the Yangzi valley have recently been recognized as sources of social experience that contributed to state formation in northern China (M. Li 2018). Their significance is measured by the degree of their stateness (cf. Renfrew and Liu 2018; Liu, Qin, and Zhuang 2020).

Instead of grappling with why and how the ancient societies of southern East Asia were derailed on their trajectory to states – or did not progress fast enough to keep up with the Central Plains – this Element explored the institutional configurations that helped people in this region to attain their goals through cooperation. Unlike organizations, such as states, institutions are defined not by their formal characteristics (e.g., territoriality, professional administrators, number of tiers in settlement hierarchy) but by their effects. Institutions of intensive cooperation achieve a high level of commitment by the participants and make possible large-scale labor projects that result in artificial landscapes, but these institutions do not necessarily correspond to state organizations. Institutions are particularly good to think with in light of the ongoing reconceptualization of early polities as volatile and fragile bundles of opportunistically repurposed preexisting practices and relations, rather than a stage in social evolution (Yoffee 2004; Campbell 2009; Graeber and Wengrow 2021).

Southern East Asians were neither natural state avoiders nor state builders who tried and failed. Populations of the Yangzi valley achieved remarkably intensive coordination within large regional groups through varying organizational arrangements, some of which meet several formal criteria of "state-level societies" (e.g., centralized authority and steep hierarchies of wealth and status), while others do not. These institutional experiments do not add up to a continuous trajectory toward the ideal type of centralized organization, the state, nor does the reduction of cooperation intensity represent a societal collapse and a start with a clean slate. Recent archaeological work suggests that the long-term continuity of regional cultures in southern East Asia was a rule rather than an exception. This Element argues that the regional populations adjusted the degree of intensive and extensive cooperation in response to changing climatic and demographic conditions, the availability of new crops and technologies, and external contacts. This scenario accounts for the accretion of institutional experience, but it does not presuppose linear progress toward a known outcome.

The divergence between the North and the South was not one of progress versus stagnation or cyclicity. Continuous institutional centralization in the Central Plains was a peculiar phenomenon, not a natural course of events, defined by the region's exposure to continuous military-technological innovation in Inner Eurasia, particularly after the middle of the second millennium BCE. North China polities became distinctively more powerful when they developed mechanisms of transregional intensive cooperation under the Western Zhou. Not coincidentally, this was also the first northern polity to carry out a planned military expansion into the Yangzi valley. These mechanisms were further perfected by the territorial states of the Eastern Zhou era, which eliminated indigenous polities along the Yangzi and promulgated, often by force, distinctively "Chinese" lifestyles among the local populations: intensive agriculture, urbanism, market-driven craft production, use of coined money, and omnipresence of the written word that, through household registration, taxation, labor mobilization, and the work of judicial machinery, affected illiterate subjects just as powerfully as the literate ones.

The Qin and Han Empires marked the apogee of state power in East Asia, which the subsequent empires in this part of the world aspired to but often struggled to achieve. But the ancient empires also were intrinsically network-based enterprises. They intensified the flows of people, goods, and information among the largely autonomous nodes and allowed privileged actors to take advantage of the improved connectivity. Although its overwhelming military power could force people to join an empire, in the longer run, it was the cost–benefit balance of participation in the imperial network that defined their decisions to either support its institutions or opt for alternative forms of trans-local cooperation, such as the "world religions" (Mann 1986: 301–40). Empires were also undermined by inadvertent consequences of environmental connectivity they enabled, such as the spread of diseases. This was the background of late antique/early medieval old-world "globalization," when the fission of classical empires powered decentralized transregional economic exchanges and the formation of peer-state systems.

There is an ongoing debate about the causes and consequences of the so-called First Great Divergence: the revival of the East Asian empire in the sixth and seventh centuries CE and the simultaneous failure of such a revival in the Mediterranean and Western Europe (Scheidel 2011). The Sui 隋 (589–618) and Tang 唐 (618–907) Empires at the peak of their power matched or surpassed the Han Empire in terms of their territory and registered population, and their unification of continental East Asia repeated the familiar pattern of centralized and militarized North conquering the weaker South.

However, the early medieval Chinese empires were not a carbon copy of their classical predecessors. The South that fell into the hands of the Sui armies in 589 was going through transformations that, over the following few centuries, turned it into the economic locomotive not only of the Chinese empire but also the emerging Afro-Eurasian world system. Land reclamation, urbanization, expansion of canal networks, and commercial boom in the Lower Yangzi, Pearl, and Red River Deltas were largely driven by private initiative. Through peer-to-peer diplomacy, trade, and Buddhist interactions, the southern river-based urban network became part of the South Seas maritime zone, which at the time experienced a connectivity revolution of its own. In the fourth and fifth centuries, Southern and Southeast Asian seafarers opened an all-sea route between the Indian Ocean and the South China Sea through the Strait of Malacca, spurring the expansion of trade into the Indonesian Archipelago (Shaffer 1996; Wang 2003). Growing markets and falling costs of transportation triggered the emergence of export-oriented, mass-producing private industries, especially in ceramics, that from the Tang period onward propelled southern China to the position of the principal manufacturing center of the Old World (Stangardt 2014).

The case of southern East Asia highlights a somewhat paradoxical pattern. The military triumphs of activist and militarized northern powers – the Qin and Han, Sui and Tang, as well as the Mongol and Manchu Empires – reinforced decentralized networks of private actors: merchants, financiers, manufacturers, and market-oriented agricultural producers, who profited from improved security, unimpeded transregional connections, and infrastructural investment brought about by the imperial unification. For much of China's late imperial era (1368–1912), the state, with its political centers and military interests in the distant North, struggled to tap the resources of this expanding economy efficiently. The distinctively southern institutional package of weakly regulated exchange networks, limited state involvement in maritime commerce, and the prevalence of private-order property enforcement and private monies set China apart from the Western European dynamics of war-driven colonial expansion, armed trade, and fiscal centralization.

References

Abu-Lughod, J. (1989). *Before European Hegemony: The World System A.D. 1250–1350*. New York: Oxford University Press.

Allard, F. (1997). Growth and stability among complex societies in prehistoric Lingnan, Southeast China. *Papers from the Institute of Archaeology*, 8, 37–58.

Allard, F. (2017). Globalization at the crossroads: The case of Southeast China during the pre- and early imperial period. In T. Hodos, ed., *The Routledge Handbook of Archaeology and Globalization*. London: Routledge, pp. 454–69.

Allard, F. (2018). The lives of shovels, vessels, and bells in early South China: Memory, ritual, and the power of destination. In F. Allard, Y. Sun, & K. Linduff, eds., *Memory and Agency in Ancient China: Shaping the Life History of Objects*. Cambridge: Cambridge University Press, pp. 50–71.

Allard, F. (2022). The Han and Three Kingdoms period burials at Hepu, China. Paper presented at the Ninth Worldwide Conference of the Society for East Asian Archaeology, Daegu, South Korea.

Anthony, D. (2007). *The Horse, the Wheel, and Language: How Bronze-Age Riders from the Eurasian Steppes Shaped the Modern World*. Princeton: Princeton University Press.

Bagley, R. (1999). Shang archaeology. In M. Loewe & E. Shaughnessy, eds., *The Cambridge History of Ancient China: From the Origins of Civilization to 221 B.C.* Cambridge: Cambridge University Press, pp. 124–231.

Ban, G. (2002). *Hanshu* [*The Documents of Han*]. 12 Vols. Beijing: Shonghua Shuju.

Bang, P. (2008). *The Roman Bazaar: A Comparative Study of Trade and Markets in a Tributary Empire*. Cambridge: Cambridge University Press.

Bang, P. (2012). Predation. In W. Scheidel, ed., *Tha Cambridge Companion to the Roman Economy*. Cambridge: Cambridge University Press, pp. 197–217.

Barbieri-Low, A. (2007). *Artisans in Early Imperial China*. Seattle: University of Washington Press.

Barbieri-Low, A. (2021). Coerced migration and resettlement in the Qin imperial expansion. *Journal of Chinese History*, 5, 181–202.

Barnes, G. (2015). *Archaeology of East Asia: The Rise of Civilization in China, Korea and Japan*. Oxford: Oxbow.

Bellina, B. (2014). Maritime Silk Roads' ornament industries: Socio-political practices and cultural transfers in the South China Sea. *Cambridge Archaeological Journal*, 24(3), 345–77.

Bellwood, P. (2013). *First Migrations: Ancient Migration in Global Perspective*. Oxford: Wiley Blackwell.

Benati, G. & Guerriero, C. (2022). The origins of the state: Technology, cooperation, and institutions. *Journal of Institutional Economics*, 18, 29–43.

Brindley, E. (2015). *Ancient China and the Yue: Perceptions and Identities on the Southern Frontier, c. 400 BCE–50 CE*. Cambridge: Cambridge University Press.

Broodbank, C. (2013). *The Making of the Middle Sea: A History of the Mediterranean from the Beginning to the Emergence of the Classical World*. London: Thames and Hudson.

Brooke, J. (2014). *Climate Change and the Course of Global History*. Cambridge: Cambridge University Press.

Campbell, R. (2009). Toward a network and boundaries approach to early complex polities: The Late Shang case. *Current Anthropology*, 50(6), 821–48.

Campbell, R. (2014a). *Archaeology of the Chinese Bronze Age from Erlitou to Anyang*. Los Angeles: UCLA Cotsen Institute of Archaeology Press.

Campbell, R. (2014b). Transformations of violence: On humanity and inhumanity in Early China. In R. Campbell, ed., *Violence and Civilization: Studies of Social Violence in History and Prehistory*. Oxford: Oxbow Books, pp. 94–118.

Campbell, R. (2018). *Violence, Kinship and the Early Chinese State: The Shang and Their World*. Cambridge: Cambridge University Press.

Campbell, R., Jaffe, Y., Kim, C., Sturm, C., & Jaang, L. (2022). Chinese Bronze Age political economies: A complex polity provisioning approach. *Journal of Archaeological Research*, 30, 69–116.

Cao, J., ed. (2022). *Wucheng Han jian* [*Han Documents from Wucheng*]. Shanghai: Shanghai Shuhua.

Carneiro, R. (1970). A theory of the origin of the state. *Science*, 39, 733–38.

Chang, K.-C. (2006). *The Archaeology of Ancient China, 4th ed*. New Haven: Yale University Press.

Chen, B. (2016). *Cong zhongxin dao bianjiang – Han diguo chengshi yu chengshi tixi de kaoguxue yanjiu* [*From the Center to the Frontiers: An Archaeological Study of Cities and City Systems in the Han Empire*]. Beijing: Kexue.

Chen, B. (2019). *Cultural Interactions during the Zhou Period (c. 1000–350 BC): A Study of Networks from the Suizao Corridor*. Oxford: Archaeopress.

Chen, K., Mei, J., Rehren, T., et al. (2019). Hanzhong bronzes and highly radiogenic lead in Shang period China. *Journal of Archaeological Science*, 101, 131–39.

Chen, M. (2022). *China and the World in the Liangzhu Era*. Singapore: Springer.

Chen, R. (2018). *Zhanguo Chu jun yanjiu* [*A Study of Chu Commanderies during the Warring States Period*]. MA thesis, Wuhan University.

Chen, W. (1989). E-jun Qi jie yu Chu guo mianshui wenti [Tallies of Qi, Lord of E, and the problem of tax exemption in the state of Chu]. *Jianghan kaogu*, 3, 52–58.

Chen, W. (1996). *Baoshan Chu jian chutan* [*A Preliminary Study of the Chu Bamboo Slips from Baoshan*]. Wuhan: Wuhan Daxue.

Childs-Johnson, E. (2019). Jade Age adornment of the Liangzhu elite. In S. Lullo & L. Wallace, eds., *The Art and Archaeology of Bodily Adornment: Studies from Central and East Asian Mortuary Context*. New York: Routledge, pp. 141–60.

Childs-Johnson, E. & Major, J. (2023). *Metamorphic Imagery in Ancient Chinese Art and Religion*. New York: Routledge.

Chiou-Peng, T. (1998). Western Yunnan and its Steppe affinities. In V. Mair, ed., *The Bronze Age and Early Iron Age Peoples of Eastern Central Asia, Volume 1: Archaeology, Migration and Nomadism, Linguistics*. Philadelphia: The Institute for the Study of Man, pp. 280–304.

Chiou-Peng, T. (2009). Incipient metallurgy in Yunnan: New data for old debates. In J. Mei & T. Rehren, eds., *Metallurgy and Civilization: Eurasia and Beyond*. London: Artchetype, pp. 79–84.

Chittick, A. (2020). *The Jiankang Empire in Chinese and World History*. Oxford: Oxford University Press.

Churchman, C. (2015). Where to draw the line? The Chinese southern frontier in the fifth and sixth centuries. In J. Anderson & J. Whitmore, eds., *China's Encounters on the South and Southwest: Reforging the Fiery Frontier over the Two Millennia*. Leiden: Brill, 59–77.

Churchman, C. (2016). *The People between the Rivers: The Rise and Fall of a Bronze Drum Culture, 200–750 CE*. Lanham: Rowman and Littlefield.

Ciarla, R. (2007). Rethinking Yuanlongpo: The case for technological links between the Lingnan (PRC) and Central Thailand in the Bronze Age. *East and West*, 57(1–4), 305–28.

Clift, P. & Plum, R. (2008). *The Asian Monsoon: Causes, History and Effects*. Cambridge: Cambridge University Press.

Cook, C. & Major, J., eds. (1999). *Defining Chu: Image and Reality in Ancient China*. Honolulu: University of Hawai'i Press.

Creel, H. (1964). The beginnings of bureaucracy in China: The origin of the *hsien*. *Journal of Asian Studies*, 22, 155–83.

Crone, P. (1989). *Pre-industrial Societies*. Oxford: Blackwell.

Crooks, P. & Parsons, T. (2016). Empires, bureaucracy and the paradox of power. In P. Crooks & T. Parsons, eds., *Empires and Bureaucracy in World History: From Late Antiquity to the Twentieth Century*. Cambridge: Cambridge University Press, 3–28.

Crossley, P. (2016). The imaginal bond of "empire" and "civilization" in Eurasian history. *Verge: Studies in Global Asias*, 2(2), 84–114.

Dai, J., Cai, X., Jin, J., et al. (2021). Earliest arrival of millet in the South China coast dating back to 5,500 years ago. *Journal of Archaeological Science*, 129, 1–9.

Dal Martello, R. (2020). Agricultural Trajectories in Yunnan, Southwest China: A Comparative Analysis of Archaeological Remains form the Neolithic to the Bronze Age. PhD thesis, University College London.

Dal Martello, R., Li, X., & Fuller, D. (2021). Two-season agriculture and irrigated rice during the Dian: Radiocarbon dates and archaeobotanical remains from Dayingzhuang, Yunnan, Southwest China. *Archaeological and Anthropological Sciences*, 13, 1–21.

Dalfes, N., Kukla, G., & Weiss, H., eds. (1997). *Third Millennium BC Climate Change and Old World Collapse*. Berlin: Springer.

D'Alpoim Guedes, J. (2011). Millets, rice, social complexity, and the spread of agriculture to the Chengdu Plain and Southwest China. *Rice*, 4, 104–13.

Demandt, M. (2015). Early gold ornaments of Southeast Asia: Production, trade, and consumption. *Asian Perspectives: The Journal of Archaeology for Asia and the Pacific*, 54(2), 305–30.

Demattè, P. (2022). *The Origins of Chinese Writing*. Oxford: Oxford University Press.

Deng, Z., Hung, H., Fan, X., Huang, Y. & Lu, H. (2018). The ancient dispersal of millets in southern China: New archaeological evidence. *The Holocene*, 28(1), 34–43.

Deopik, D. & Ulyanov, M. (2011). Sovremennije dannije o drevnejshikh pismennostiakh v Vostochnoj Azii i sviazannije s nimi znaki i teksti (The new evidence for the ancient writing systems in East Asia and related signs and texts). *Voprosi epigrafiki* [*Studies in Epigraphy*], 5, 7–118.

Derevyanko, A., ed. (2016). *Istorija Kitaja s drevnejshikh vremen do nachala XXI veka* [*History of China from Prehistory to the Beginning of the Twenty-First Century*], *Volume 1: Drevnejshaja i drevniaja istorija* [*Prehistory and Early History*]. Moscow: Nauka–Vostochnaja Literatura.

Duan, C., Gan, X., Wang, J., & Chien, P. (1998). Relocation of civilization centers in ancient China: Environmental factors. *Ambio*, 27(7), 572–75.

Ehrich, R. (2017). The Culture Problem in Neolithic Archaeology: Examples and Possible Solutions in the Middle Yangzi River Region. PhD thesis, University of California, Los Angeles.

Emura, H. (2011). *Shunshū Sengoku jidai seidō kahei no seisei to tenkai* [*Emergence and Development of Bronze Coinage during the Spring and Autumn and Warring States Periods*]. Tokyo: Kyūko Shoin.

Erickson, S., Yi, S., & Nylan, M. (2010). The archaeology of outlying lands. In M. Nylan & M. Loewe, eds., *China's Early Empires: A Re-appraisal*. Cambridge: Cambridge University Press, pp. 135–68.

Falkenhausen, L. von (1996). The Moutuo bronzes: New perspectives on the Late Bronze Age in Sichuan. *Arts Asiatiques*, 51, 29–59.

Falkenhausen, L. von (2002). The use and significance of ritual bronzes in the Lingnan region during the Eastern Zhou Period. *Journal of East Asian Archaeology*, 3(1–2), 193–236.

Falkenhausen, L. von (2003). Social ranking in Chu tombs: The mortuary background of the Warring States manuscript finds. *Monumenta Serica*, 51, 439–526.

Falkenhausen, L. von (2005). The E Jun Qi metal tallies: Inscribed texts and ritual contexts. In M. Kern, ed., *Text and Ritual in Early China*. Seattle: University of Washington Press, pp. 79–123.

Falkenhausen, L. von (2006a). *Chinese Society in the Age of Confucius (1000–250 BC): The Archaeological Evidence*. Los Angeles: Cotsen Institute of Archaeology, UCLA.

Falkenhausen, L. von (2006b). The external connections of Sanxingdui. *Journal of Eats Asian Archaeology*, 5(1–4), 191–245.

Falkenhausen, L. von (2011). The Bronze Age of the upper Han River basin: Some observations. In W. Cao, ed., *Hanzhong chutu Shang dai qingtongqi* [*Shang-Period Bronzes Unearthed at Hanzhong*]. Chengdu: Bashu, pp. 378–516.

Falkenhausen, L. von (2018). The economic role of cities in Eastern Zhou China. *Archaeological Research in Asia*, 14, 161–69.

Falkenhausen, L. von (2022). The economy of late pre-imperial China: Archaeological perspectives. In D. Ma & R. Von Glahn, eds., *The*

Cambridge Economic History of China, Volume 1: To 1800. Cambridge: Cambridge University Press, pp. 15–51.

Fan, Y. (1965). *Hou Hanshu* [*The Documents of Later Han*]. 10 Vols. Beijing: Shonghua Shuju.

Fang, Q. (2018). *Zeng guo lishi yu wenhua: cong "zuo you Wen Wu" dao "zuo you Chu wang"* [*History and Culture of the State of Zeng: From "Assisting Kings Wen and Wu" to "Assisting the King of Chu"*]. Shanghai: Shanghai Guji.

Feinman, G., Nicholas, L., & Hui, F. (2010). The imprint of China's First Emperor on the distant realm of eastern Shandong. *Proceedings of the National Academy of Sciences of the United States of America*, 107(11), 4851–56.

Feng, P. (2007). *Wu Yue wenhua* [*The Wu and Yue Culture*]. Beijing: Wenwu.

Flad, R. (2008). Divination and power: A multiregional view of the development of oracle bone divination in Early China. *Current Anthropology*, 49(3), 403–37.

Flad, R. (2011). *Salt Production and Social Hierarchy in Ancient China: An Archaeological Investigation of Specialization in China's Three Gorges*. New York: Cambridge University Press.

Flad, R. (2013). The Sichuan Basin Neolithic. In A. Underhill, ed., *A Companion to Chinese Archaeology*. Chichester: Wiley-Blackwell, pp. 125–46.

Flad, R. & Chen, P. (2013). *Ancient Central China: Centers and Peripheries along the Yangzi River*. Cambridge: Cambridge University Press.

Fuller, D., Qin, L., & Harvey, E. (2008). Evidence for a late onset of agriculture in the Lower Yangtze region and challenges for an archaeobotany of rice. In A. Sanchez-Mazas, R. Blench, M. Ross, I. Peiros, & M. Lin, eds., *Past Human Migrations in East Asia: Matching Archaeology, Linguistics and Genetics*. London: Routledge, pp. 40–83.

Gao, Z. (1984). Zhongguo nanfang chutu Shang Zhou tongnao gailun [A discussion of Shang and Zhou-period bronze *nao* bells excavated in southern China]. *Hunan kaogu jikan*, 2, 128–35.

Gao, Z. (2012). *Hunan Chu mu yu Chu wenhua* [*Chu Tombs and Chu Culture in Hunan*]. Changsha: Yuelu Shushe.

Ge, J. (2000). *Zhongguo renkou shi* [*The Population History of China*]. Shanghai: Fudan Daxue.

Ge, J. (2004). *Zhongguo gudai de ditu cehui* [*Mapmaking in Ancient China*]. Beijing: Shangwu Yinshuguan.

Gernet, J. (1995). *Buddhism in Chinese Society: An Economic History from the Fifth to the Tenth Centuries*. New York: Columbia University Press.

Graeber, D. & Wengrow, D. (2021). *The Dawn of Everything: A New History of Humanity.* London: Allen Lane.

Guangzhou shi wenwu kaogu yanjiusuo, Zhongguo shehui kexueyuan kaogu yanjiusuo, & Nanyue wang bowuyuan (2022). *Nanyue mujian* [*Wooden Slips from Nanyue*]. Beijing: Wenwu.

Guo, J. (2013). *Xia Shang Zhou: cong shenhua dao shishi* [*Xia, Shang, and Zhou: From Myth to History*]. Shanghai: Shanghai Guji.

Guo, J. & Sturm, C. (2022). Water, earth, and fire: The making of riverine communities in the greater Jiang Han Region of Central China (4th–3rd millennia BCE). In T. Wynn, ed., *The Oxford Handbook of Cognitive Archaeology.* Oxford: Oxford University Press, 949–78.

Haldon, J. (2021). The political economy of empire: "Imperial capital" and the formation of central and regional elites. In P. Bang, C. A. Bayly, & W. Scheidel, eds., *The Oxford World History of Empire, Volume One: The Imperial Experience*. Oxford: Oxford University Press, pp. 179–220.

He, J. (2004). *Mawangdui Han mu* [*Han Tombs at Mawangdui*]. Beijing: Wenwu.

Hein, A. (2022). Culture contacts in ancient worlds: A review of theoretical debates and practical applications. *Journal of World History*, 33(4), 541–79.

Hermans, E., ed. (2020). *A Companion to the Global Early Middle Ages*. Leeds: Arc Humanities Press.

Higham, C. (2014). *Early Mainland Southeast Asia: From First Humans to Angkor.* Bangkok: River Books.

Higham, C. (2019). A maritime route brought first farmers to mainland Southeast Asia. In C. Wu & B. Rolett, eds., *Prehistoric Maritime Culture and Seafaring in East Asia*. Singapore: Springer, pp. 41–52.

Higham, C. (2021). The later prehistory of Southeast Asia and Southern China: The impact of exchange, farming and metallurgy. *Asian Archaeology*, 4, 63–93.

Higham, C., Higham, T., Ciarla, R., et al. (2011). The origins of the Bronze Age of Southeast Asia. *Journal of World Prehistory*, 24, 227–74.

Higham, T., Weiss, A., Higham, C., et al. (2020). A prehistoric copper-production centre in Central Thailand: Its dating and wider implications. *Antiquity*, 94, 948–65.

Hopkins, K. (1980). Taxes and trade in the Roman Empire (200 B.C. – A.D. 400). *The Journal of Roman Studies*, 70, 101–25.

Hsu, C.-Y. (1965). *Ancient China in Transition: An Analysis of Social Mobility, 722–222 B.C.* Stanford: Stanford University Press.

Hsu, Y.-K., O'Sullivan, R., & Li, H. (2021). Sources of Western Zhou lead: A new understanding of Chinese Bronze Age supply network. *Archaeological and Anthropological Sciences*, 13, 1–15.

Hu, X. (2015). *Huangshi wenhua yichan* [*The Cultural Legacy of Huangshi Municipality*]. Wuhan: Changjiang.

Huan, L. (2023). *How Leaded Bronze Transformed China, 2000–1000 BCE*. Oxford: BAR.

Huang, Z. (2015). *Nanyue kaoguxue yanjiu* [*An Archaeological Study of Nanyue*]. Beijing: Zhongguo Shehui Kexue.

Hudson, M. (2022). *Bronze Age Maritime and Warrior Dynamics in Island East Asia*. Cambridge: Cambridge University Press.

Hunan sheng wenwu kaogu yanjiusuo (2006). *Liye fajue baogao* [*Report on the Excavation at Liye*]. Changsha: Yuelu Shushe.

Hunan sheng wenwu kaogu yanjiusuo, Changsha shi kaogu yanjiusuo, & Ningxiang xian wenwu guanlisuo (2006). Hunan Ningxiang Tanheli Xi Zhou chengzhi yu muzang fajue jianbao [Preliminary report on the excavation of the Western Zhou town and burials at Tanheli, Ningxiang, Hunan]. *Wenwu*, 6, 4–35.

Jaang, L. (2015). The landscape of China's participation in the Bronze Age Eurasian network. *Journal of World Prehistory*, 28, 179–213.

Jaffe, Y., Campbell, R., & Shelach-Lavi, G. (2022). Shimao and the rise of states in China: Archaeology, historiography, and myth. *Current Anthropology*, 63(1), 95–117.

Jaffe, Y. & Hein, A. (2021). Considering change with archaeological data: Reevaluating local variation in the role of the -4.2 k BP event in Northwest China. *The Holocene*, 31(2), 169–82.

Jennings, J. (2011). *Globalizations and the Ancient World*. Cambridge: Cambridge University Press.

Jiangxi sheng wenwu kaogu yanjiusuo, Jiangxi sheng bowuguan, & Xin'gan xian bowuguan (1997). *Xin'gan Shang dai da mu* [*A Great Shang-Period Tomb at Xin'gan*]. Beijing: Wenwu.

Jiangxi sheng wenwu kaogu yanjiusuo & Zhangshu shi bowuguan (2005). *Wucheng: 1973–2002 nian kaogu fajue baogao* [*Wucheng: Archaeological Report on the Excavations of 1973–2002*]. Beijing: Kexue.

Jin, Z., Liu, R., Rawson, J., & Pollard, M. (2017). Revising lead isotope data in Shang and Western Zhou bronzes. *Antiquity*, 91, 1574–87.

Khayutina, M. (2017). Kinship, Marriage and Politics in Early China (13–8 c. BCE) in the Light of Ritual Bronze Inscriptions. Habilitation thesis, University of Munich.

Kim, N. (2015). *The Origins of Ancient Vietnam*. Oxford: Oxford University Press.

Kiser, E. & Cai, Y. (2003). War and bureaucratization in Qin China: Exploring an anomalous case. *American Sociological Review*, 68, 511–39.

Kohl, P. (2007). *The Making of Bronze Age Eurasia*. Cambridge: Cambridge University Press.

Korolkov, M. (2021). Fiscal transformation during the formative period of ancient Chinese empire (late fourth to first century BCE). In J. Valk & I. Soto Marín, eds., *Ancient Taxation: The Mechanics of Extraction in Comparative Perspective*. New York: New York University Press, pp. 203–61.

Korolkov, M. (2022). *The Imperial Network in Ancient China: The Foundation of Sinitic Empire in Southern East Asia*. London: Routledge.

Korolkov, M. (2023a). Building empire, creating markets: Commercial policies and practices in imperial Qin (221–207 BCE). *Journal of the Economic and Social History of the Orient*, 66, 206–36.

Korolkov, M. (2023b). Southern sea ports of the Han Empire: Urbanization and trade in coastal Lingnan, 300 BCE–300 CE. In S. von Reden, ed., *Handbook of Ancient Afro-Eurasian Economies, Volume 3: Frontier-Zone Processes and Transimperial Exchange*. Berlin: De Gruyter, pp. 295–337.

Korolkov, M. & Hein, A. (2021). State-induced migration and the creation of state spaces in early Chinese empires: Perspectives from history and archaeology. *Journal of Chinese History*, 5, 203–25.

Lai, C. (2019). *Contacts between the Shang and the South c. 1300–1045 BC: Resemblance and Resistance*. Oxford: BAR.

Lam, W. (2020). Iron technology and its regional development during the Eastern Zhou period. In E. Childs-Johnson, ed., *The Oxford Handbook of Early China*. Oxford: Oxford University Press, pp. 595–614.

Lam, W. (2023). *Connectivity, Imperialism, and the Han Iron Industry*. London: Routledge.

Lam, W., Zhang, Q., Chen, J., & Wu S. (2020). Provision of iron objects in the southern borderlands of the Han Empire: A metallurgical study of iron objects from Han tombs in Guangzhou. *Archaeological and Anthropological Series*, 12, 1–22.

Lander, B. (2014). State management of river dikes in Early China: New sources on the environmental history of the Central Yangzi region. *T'oung Pao*, 100(4–5), 325–62.

Lander, B. (2021). *The King's Harvest: A Political Ecology of China from the First Farmers to the First Empire*. New Haven: Yale University Press.

Lander, B. (2022a). From wetland to farmland: How humans transformed the Central Yangzi Basin. *Asia Major*, 35(1), 1–31.

Lander, B. (2022b). Deforestation in Early China: How people adapted to wood scarcity. In I. Miller, B. Davis, B. Lander, & J. Lee, eds., *The Cultivated Forest: People and Woodlands in Asian History*. Seattle: University of Washington Press, pp. 1–19.

Laptev, S. (2011). The origin and development of the Wucheng Culture (in the context of intercultural contacts between Bronze Age inhabitants of the lower Yangzi valley and Indochina Peninsula). *Archaeology, Ethnology and Anthropology of Eurasia*, 38(4), 93–102.

Lee, C., Qi, S., Zhang, G., et al. (2008). Seven thousand years of records on the mining and utilization of metals from lake sediments in Central China. *Environmental Science and Technology*, 42(13), 4732–38.

Lewis, M. (1990). *Sanctioned Violence in Early China*. Albany: State University of New York Press.

Lewis, M. (1999). Warring States political history. In M. Loewe & E. Shaughnessy, eds., *The Cambridge History of Ancient China: From the Origins of Civilization to 221 B.C.* Cambridge: Cambridge University Press, pp. 587–650.

Lewis, M. (2007). *The Early Chinese Empires: Qin and Han*. Cambridger, MA: Harvard University Press.

Li, F. (2008). *Bureaucracy and the State in Early China: Governing the Western Zhou*. Cambridge: Cambridge University Press.

Li, F. (2013). *Early China: A Social and Cultural History*. Cambridge: Cambridge University Press.

Li, F. (2018). The development of literacy in Early China: With the nature and uses of bronze inscriptions in context, and more. In A. Kolb, ed., *Literacy in Ancient Everyday Life*. Berlin: De Gruyter.

Li, H., Chen, J., Cui, J., et al. (2020). Production and circulation of bronzes among the regional states in the Western Zhou Dynasty. *Journal of Archaeological Science*, 121, 1–15.

Li, L. (2010). Lingnan diqu chutu de Handai xunlu ji xunxiang xisu qiyuan qianyi [Some remarks on the Han-period censers excavated in the Lingnan region and the custom of incense burning]. In Zhongguo shehui kexueyuan kaogu yanjiusuo & Guangzhou shi wenwu kaogu yanjiusuo, eds., *Xi Han Nanyue guo kaogu yu Han wenhua* [*Archaeology of the Western Han State of Nanyue and the Han Culture*]. Beijing: Kexue, pp. 164–76.

Li, M. (2018). *Social Memory and State Formation in Early China*. Cambridge: Cambridge University Press.

Li, M. (2019). Why early cities failed: Fragility and resilience in Bronze Age China. In N. Yoffee, ed., *The Evolution of Fragility: Setting the Terms*. Cambridge: McDonald Institute for Archaeological Research, pp. 25–45.

Li, M., Roberts, C., Chen, L., & Zhao, D. (2019). A male adult skeleton from the Han Dynasty in Shaanxi, China (202 BC – 220 AD) with bone changes that possibly represent spinal tuberculosis. *International Journal of Paleopathology*, 27, 9–16.

Li, T. (2015). Swamps, lakes, rivers and elephants: A preliminary attempt towards an environmental history of the Red River Delta, c. 600–1400. *Water History*, 7, 199–211.

Li, X. (1991). Chu bronzes and Chu culture. In T. Lawton, ed., *New Perspectives on Chu Culture during the Eastern Zhou period*. Princeton: Princeton University Press, pp. 1–22.

Li, Y. (2019). Preliminary analysis of the development of Neolithic culture in coastal region of Guangdong. In C. Wu & B. Rolett, eds., *Prehistoric Maritime Culture and Seafaring in East Asia*. Singapore: Springer, pp. 103–26.

Lieberman, V. (2008). Protected rimlands and exposed zones: Reconfiguring premodern Eurasia. *Comparative Studies in Society and History*, 50(3), 692–723.

Lin, G. (2017). *Qin zheng Nan Yue lungao* [*On the Qin Conquest of the Southern Yue*]. Guangzhou: Guangdong Renmin.

Linduff, K. (2018). Technoscapes and the materialization of ideas in metal on the Inner Asian frontier (c. 3000–1500 BCE). In K. Linduff, Y. Sun, W. Cao, & Y. Liu, eds., *Ancient China and Its Eurasian Neighbors: Artifacts, Identity and Death in the Frontier, 3000–700 BCE*. Cambridge: Cambridge University Press, pp. 35–71.

Liu, B., Wang, N., Chen, M., et al. (2018). Earliest hydraulic enterprise in China, 5,100 years ago. *Proceedings of the National Academy of Sciences of the United States of America*, 114(52), 13637–42.

Liu, B., Qin, L., & Zhuang, Y., eds. (2020). *Liangzhu Culture: Society, Belief, and Art in Neolithic China*. London and New York: Routledge.

Liu, B., Wang, N., & Chen, M. (2020). The Liangzhu city: New discoveries and research. In B. Liu, Qin, L., & Zhuang, Y., eds., *Liangzhu Culture: Society, Belief, and Art in Neolithic China*. London: Routledge, pp. 18–48.

Liu, J. (2023). *Jianghan pingyuan shiqian zhishui wenming* [*Prehistoric Hydraulic Civilization of the Jianghan Plain*]. Beijing: Zhongguo Shehui Kexue.

Liu, L. (2003). "The products of minds as well as hands": Production of prestige goods in the Neolithic and Early State periods of China. *Asian Perspectives*, 42(1), 1–40.

Liu, L. (2004). *The Chinese Neolithic: Trajectories to Early States*. Cambridge: Cambridge University Press.

Liu, L. & Chen, X. (2001). Cities and towns: The control of natural resources in early states. *Bulletin of the Museum of Far Eastern Antiquities*, 73, 5–47.

Liu, L. & Chen, X. (2003). *State Formation in Early China*. London: Duckworth.

Liu, L. & Chen, X. (2012). *The Archaeology of China: From the Late Paleolithic to the Early Bronze Age*. Cambridge: Cambridge University Press.

Liu, R. (2019). *Qin Han diguo nanyuan de mianxiang: yi kaogu shijiao de shenshi* [*The Southern Fringes of the Qin and Han Empires: An Archaeological Investigation*]. Beijing: Zhongguo Shehui Kexue.

Liu, R., Rawson, J., & Pollard, M. (2018). Beyond ritual bronzes: Identifying multiple sources of highly radiogenic lead across Chinese history. *Scientific Reports*, 8, 1–7.

Liu, R., Pollard, M., Rawson, J., et al. (2019). Panlongcheng, Zhengzhou and the movement of metal in Early Bronze Age China. *Journal of World Prehistory*, 32, 393–428.

Liu, S. (2019). The southern economy. In A. Dien & K. Knapp, eds., *The Cambridge History of China, Volume 2: The Six Dynasties, 220–589*. Cambridge: Cambridge University Press, pp. 330–54.

Liu, T., Chen, Z., Sun, Q., & Finlayson, B. (2011). Migration of Neolithic settlement in the Dongting Lake area of the middle Yangtze River basin: Lake-level and monsoon climate responses. *The Holocene*, 22(6), 649–57.

Liu, X. (2017). *Xian Qin liang Han nongye yu xiangcun juluo de kaoguxue yanjiu* [*An Archaeological Study of Agriculture and Rural Settlement during the Pre-Qin and Han Periods*]. Beijing: Wenwu.

Mann, M. (1986). *The Sources of Social Power, Volume 1: A History of Power from the Beginning to A.D. 1760*. Cambridge: Cambridge University Press.

Marks, R. (2004). *Tigers, Rice, Silk, and Silt: Environment and Economy in Late Imperial South China*. Cambridge: Cambridge University Press.

Marks, R. (2012). *China: Its Environment and History*. Lanham: Rowman and Littlefield.

McConnel, J., Wilson, A., Stohl, A., & Steffensen, J. (2018). Lead pollution recorded in Greenland ice indicates European emissions tracked plagues, wars, and imperial expansion during antiquity. *Proceedings of the National Academy of Sciences*, 115(22), 5726–31.

McNeal, R. (2014). Erligang contacts south of the Yangzi River: The expansion of interaction networks in Early Bronze Age Hunan. In K. Steinke & D. Ching, eds., *Art and Archaeology of the Erligang Civilization*. Princeton: Princeton University Press, pp. 173–87.

McNeil, W. (1976). *Plagues and Peoples*. New York: Anchor Books.

Mei, J. (2003). Cultural interaction between China and Central Asia during the Bronze Age. *Proceedings of the British Academy*, 121, 1–39.

Mei, J. (2009). Early metallurgy and socio-cultural complexity: Archaeological discoveries in northwest China. In B. Hanks & K. Linduff, eds., *Social Complexity in Prehistoric Eurasia: Monuments, Metals, and Mobility*. Cambridge: Cambridge University Press, pp. 215–32.

Milburn, O. (2010). *The Glory of Yue: An Annotated Translation of the* Yuejue shu. Leiden: Brill.

Morris, I. (2003). *The Measure of Civilization: How Social Development Decides the Fate of Nations*. Princeton: Princeton University Press.

Morris, I. (2014). *War! What Is It Good For? The Role of Conflict in Civilization, from Primates to Robots*. London: Profile Books.

Müller, S. (2004). Gräber in Guangdong während der Zhanguo-Zeit. In S. Müller, T. Höllmann, & P. Gui, eds., *Guangdong: Archaeology and Early Texts/ Archäologie und frühe Texte (Zhou-Tang)*. Wiesbaden: Harrassowitz, pp. 23–49.

Murowchick, R. (2001). The political and ritual significance of bronze production and use in ancient Yunnan. *Journal of East Asian Archaeology*, 3(1–2), 133–92.

Nakamura, S. (1997). Sekikaka iseki wo aguru sho mondai [Problems related to the Shijiahe settlement remains]. *Nihon Chūgoku kōko gakkai kaihō*, 7, 41–45.

Nasu, H. (2012). Land-use change for rice and foxtail millet cultivation in the Chengtoushan site, Central China, reconstructed from weed seed assemblages. *Archaeological and Anthropological Sciences*, 4(1), 1–14.

Needham, J., Kerr, R., & Wood, N. (2004). *Science and Civilization in China, Volume 5: Chemistry and Chemical Technology, Part 12: Ceramic Technology*. Cambridge: Cambridge University Press.

Needham, J. & Wagner, D. (2008). *Science and Civilization in China, Volume 5: Chemistry and Chemical Technology, Part 11: Ferrous Metallurgy*. Cambridge: Cambridge University Press.

North, D. (1990). *Institutions, Institutional Change and Economic Performance*. Cambridge: Cambridge University Press.

Novozhenov, V. (2012). *Chudo kommunikazii i drevnejshij kolesnij transport Evrazii* [*Communications and Earliest Wheeled Transport of Eurasia*]. Moskow: TAUS.

Owen, S., ed. and transl. (1996). *An Anthology of Chinese Literature: Beginnings to 1911*. New York: W.W. Norton.

Pang, X. (2018). Routes of Communication between Erlitou Culture and the Southern Region in Bronze Age China. Early China Seminar lecture series, Columbia University.

Pang, X. & Gao, J. (2020). Shilun Erlitou wenhua shiqi Luoyang pendi he Jianghan pingyuan de jiaoliu tongdao [On the communication routes between the Luoyang Basin and the Jianghan Plain during the Erlitou-Culture period]. *Nanfang wenwu*, 2, 38–48.

Pei, A. (2013). The Pengtoushan Culture in the Middle Yangzi River valley. In A. Underhill, ed., *A Companion to Chinese Archaeology*. Chichester: Wiley-Blackwell, pp. 497–509.

Pei, A. (2020). *A Study of Prehistoric Settlement Patterns in China*. Singapore: Springer.

Peng, K. (2000). Coinage and Commercial Development in Eastern Zhou China. PhD thesis, University of Chicago.

Pollard, M., Bray, P., Hommen, P., et al. (2017). Bronze Age metal circulation in China. *Antiquity*, 91, 674–87.

Pomeranz, K. (2000). *The Great Divergence: China, Europe, and the Making of the Modern World Economy*. Princeton: Princeton University Press.

Preiser-Kapeller, J. (2018). *Jenseits von Rom und Karl dem Grossen: Aspekte der globalen Verflechtung in der langen Spätantike*. Wien: Mandelbaum.

Price, B. (1978). Secondary state formation: An explanatory model. In R. Cohen & E. Service, eds., *Origins of the State: The Anthropology of Political Evolution*. Philadelphia: Institute for the Study of Huma Issues, pp. 161–86.

Priewe, S. (2012). Social Change along the Middle Yangzi: Re-configurations of Late Neolithic Society. PhD thesis, University of Oxford.

Priewe, S. (2018). The whole and fragmented lives of jade objects from Late Neolithic Middle Yangzi River burials (c. 2000 BCE). In F. Allard, Y. Sun, & K. Linduff, eds., *Memory and Agency in Ancient China: Shaping the Life History of Objects*. Cambridge: Cambridge University Press, pp. 72–96.

Prüch, M., ed. (1999). *Schätze für Zhao Mo: Das Grab von Nan Yue*. Heidelberg: Braus.

Qin, L. (2013). The Liangzhu Culture. In A. Underhill, ed., *A Companion to Chinese Archaeology*. Chichester: Wiley-Blackwell, pp. 574–96.

Qin, L. & Fuller, D. (2019). Why rice farmers don't sail: Coastal subsistence and maritime trends in Early China. In C. Wu & B. Rolett, eds., *Prehistoric Maritime Culture and Seafaring in East Asia*. Singapore: Springer, pp. 159–91.

Qiu, X. (2000). *Chinese Writing*. Berkeley: The Society for the Study of Early China.

Rawson, J. (1999). Western Zhou archaeology. In M. Loewe & E. Shaughnessy, eds., *The Cambridge History of Ancient China: From the Origins of Civilization to 221 B.C.* Cambridge: Cambridge University Press, pp. 352–449.

Rawson, J. (2015). Steppe warriors in ancient China and the role of hand-to-hand combat. *Gugong xueshu jikan*, 33(1), 37–97.

Rawson, J. (2017). China and the steppe: Reception and resistance. *Antiquity*, 91, 375–88.

Rawson, J. (2023). *Life and Afterlife in Ancient China*. London: Penguin.

Rawson, J., Huan, L., & Taylor, W. (2021). Seeking horses: Allies, clients and exchanges in the Zhou period (1045–221 BC). *Journal of World Prehistory*, 34, 489–530.

Renfrew, C. & Liu, B. (2018). The emergence of complex society in China: The case of Liangzhu. *Antiquity*, 92, 975–90.

Roberts, N. (1989). *The Holocene: An Environmental History*. Oxford: Blackwell.

Rolett, B., Zheng, Z., & Yue, Y. (2011). Holocene sea-level change and the emergence of Neolithic seafaring in the Fuzhou Basin (Fujian, China). *Quarterly Science Reviews*, 30, 788–97.

Routledge, B. (2014). *Archaeology and State Theory: Subjects and Objects of Power*. London: Bloomsbury.

Ruddiman, W. (2003). The anthropogenic greenhouse era began thousands of years ago. *Climatic Change*, 61, 261–93.

Sagart, L. (2005). Sino-Tibetan – Austronesian: An updated and improved argument. In L. Sagart, R. Blench, & A. Sanchez-Mazas, eds., *The Peopling of East Asia: Putting Together Archaeology, Linguistics and Genetics*. London: Routledge, pp. 161–76.

Sage, S. (1992). *Ancient Sichuan and the Unification of China*. Albany: State University of New York Press.

Sanft, C. (2019). *Literate Community in Early Imperial China: The Northwestern Frontier in Han Times*. Albany: State University of New York Press.

Sanxingdui Museum (2006). *The Sanxingdui Site: Mystical Mask on Ancient Shu Kingdom*. Beijing: China Intercontinental Press.

Schafer, E. (1967). *The Vermilion Bird: T'ang Images of the South*. Berkeley: University of California Press.

Scheidel, W. (2009). In search of Roman economic growth. *Journal of Roman Archaeology*, 22, 46–70.

Scheidel, W. (2011). Fiscal regimes and the "First Great Divergence" between Eastern and Western Eurasia. In P. Bang & C. A. Bayly, eds., *Tributary Empires in Global History*. New York: Palgrave Macmillan, pp. 193–204.

Scheidel, W. (2013). Studying the state. In P. Bang & W. Scheidel, eds., *The Oxford Handbook of the State in the Ancient Near East and Mediterranean*. Oxford: Oxford University Press, pp. 5–58.

Scott, J. (2009). *The Art of Not Being Governed: An Anarchist History of Upland Southeast Asia*. New Haven: Yale University Press.

Scott, J. (2017). *Against the Grain: A Deep History of the Earliest States*. New Haven: Yale University Press.

Shaffer, L. (1996). *Maritime Southeast Asia to 1500*. Armonk: M.E. Sharpe.

Shang, X. (2003). Xi Han renkou yanjiu [A Study of Western Han Population]. PhD thesis, Zhengzhou University.

Shelach-Lavi, G. (2015). *The Archaeology of Early China: From Prehistory to the Han Dynasty*. Cambridge: Cambridge University Press.

Shelach-Lavi, G. (2018a). Main issues in the study of the Chinese Neolithic. In P. Goldin, ed., *Routledge Handbook of Early Chinese History*. London: Routledge, pp. 15–38.

Shelach-Lavi, G. (2018b). Memory, amnesia and the formation of identity symbols in China. In F. Allard, Y. Sun, & K. Linduff, eds., *Memory and Agency in Ancient China: Shaping the Life History of Objects*. Cambridge: Cambridge University Press, pp. 28–49.

Sima, Q. (2006). *Shiji* [*The Grand Scribe's Records*]. 10 Vols. Beijing: Shonghua Shuju.

Simić, K. (2018). The Byzantine Augustus: The reception of the first Roman emperor in the Byzantine tradition. In P. Goodman, ed., *Afterlives of Augustus, AD 14–2014*. Cambridge: Cambridge University Press, pp. 122–37.

Song, Z. (2008). *Shu wenhua* [*The Shu Culture*]. Beijing: Wenwu.

Sørensen, P. (1972). The Neolithic cultures of Thailand (and North Malaysia) and their Longshanoid relationship. In N. Barnard, ed., *Early Chinese Art and Its Possible Influence in the Pacific Basin*. New York: Intercultural Arts Press, pp. 459–506.

Stangardt, J. (2014). Indian Ocean trade in the ninth and tenth centuries: Demand, distance, and profit. *South Asian Studies*, 30(1), 35–55.

Steinke, K. (2014). Erligang and the southern bronze industries. In K. Steinke & D. Ching, eds., *Art and Archaeology of the Erligang Civilization*. Princeton: Princeton University Press, pp. 151–70.

Stevens, C. & Fuller, D. (2017). The spread of agriculture in Eastern Asia: Archaeological bases for hypothetical farmer/language dispersal. *Language Dynamics and Change*, 7, 152–86.

Sturm, C. (2017). Structure and Evolution of Economic Networks in Neolithic Walled Towns of the Jianghan Plain: A Geochemical Perspective. PhD thesis, University of Pittsburgh.

Sun, G. (2013). Resent research on the Hemudu Culture and the Tianluoshan site. In A. Underhill, ed., *A Companion to Chinese Archaeology*. Chichester: Wiley-Blackwell, pp. 555–73.

Sun, H. (2013). The Sanxingdui Culture of the Sichuan Basin. In A. Underhill, ed., *A Companion to Chinese Archaeology*. Chichester: Wiley-Blackwell, pp. 147–68.

Sun, J. (2008). *Handai wuzhi wenhua ziliao tushuo* [*Images and a Discussion of the Material Culture of the Han Period*]. Shanghai: Shanghai Guji.

Sun, T. (2003). Yuanshi ciqi de faming jiqi lichengbei yiyi [The invention of protoporcelain and its historic significance]. *Zhongguo taoci*, 39(3), 60–62.

Sun, Y. (2018). A divergent life history of bronze willow-leaf-shaped swords of Western Zhou China from the eleventh to the tenth century BCE. In F. Allard, Y. Sun, & K. Linduff, eds., *Memory and Agency in Ancient China: Shaping the Life History of Objects*. Cambridge: Cambridge University Press, pp. 120–51.

Sun, Y. (2021). *Many Worlds under One Heaven: Material Culture, Identity, and Power in the Northern Frontier of the Western Zhou, 1045–771 BCE*. New York: Columbia University Press.

Tainter, J. (1988). *The Collapse of Complex Societies*. Cambridge: Cambridge University Press.

Takamura, T. (2019). Sengoku Shin no "teikoku" ka to shūen ryōiki tōchi no hensen ["Imperialization" of Qin during the Warring States era and changes in territorial control at the frontiers]. In T. Takamura, ed., *Shūen ryōiki kara mita Shin Kan teikoku* [*Frontier Perspective on the Qin and Han Empires*]. Tokyo: Rokuichi Shobō, pp. 51–66.

Talhelm, T., Zhang, X., Oishi, S., et al. (2014). Large-scale psychological differences within China explained by rice versus wheat agriculture. *Science*, 344, 603–8.

Tanabe, S., Hori, K., Saito, Y., et al. (2003). Song Hong (Red River) Delta evolution related to millennium-scale Holocene sea-level changes. *Quarterly Science Reviews*, 22, 2345–61.

Taylor, K. (1983). *The Birth of Vietnam*. Berkeley: University of California Press.

Taylor, M. (2020). *Soldiers and Silver: Mobilizing Resources in the Age of Roman Conquest*. Austin: University of Texas Press.

Terpstra, T. (2019). *Trade in the Ancient Mediterranean: Private Order and Public Institutions*. Princeton: Princeton University Press.

Terrenato, N. (2007). The essential countryside of the Roman world. In S. Alcock & R. Osborne, eds., *Classical Archaeology*. Oxford: Blackwell, pp. 139–61.

Tilly, C. (1975). Reflections on the history of European state-making. In C. Tilly, ed., *The Formation of National States in Western Europe*. Princeton: Princeton University Press, pp. 3–83.

Tilly, C. (1990). *Coercion, Capital, and European States, A.D. 990–1990*. Cambridge: Basil Blackwell.

Underhill, A. & Habu, J. (2006). Early communities in East Asia: Economic and sociopolitical organization at the local and regional levels. In M. Stark, ed., *Archaeology of Asia*. Oxford: Blackwell, pp. 121–48.

Vandkilde, H. (2016). Bronzization: The Bronze Age as pre-modern globalization. *Praehistorische Zeitschrift*, 91(1), 103–23.

Venture, O. (2017). Zeng: The rediscovery of a forgotten state. In G. Kósa, ed., *China across the Centuries: Papers from a Lecture Series in Budapest*. Budapest: Department of East Asian Studies, Eötvös Loránd University, pp. 1–32.

Vogelsang, K. (2016). Getting the terms right: Political realism, politics, and the state in ancient China. *Oriens Extremus*, 55, 39–72.

Vogt, P. N. (2020). Western Zhou government and society. In E. Childs-Johnson, ed., *The Oxford Handbook of Early China*. Oxford: Oxford University Press, pp. 401–35.

Vogt, P. N. (2023). *Kingship, Ritual, and Royal Ideology in Western Zhou China*. Cambridge: Cambridge University Press.

Von Glahn, R. (2016). *The Economic History of China: From Antiquity to the Nineteenth Century*. Cambridge: Cambridge University Press.

Wan, J. (2020). *Cong Sanxingdui yizhi kan Chengdu pingyuan wenming jincheng* [*The Rise of Social Complexity on the Chengdu Plain: A View from Sanxingdui*]. Beijing: Kexue.

Wang, C. (2019). Ganjiang liuyu Shang shiqi wenhua geju bianqian [Changing cultural landscape of the Gan River valley during the Shang period]. *Kaogu yanjiu*, 2, 53–59.

Wang, G. (2003). *Nanhai Trade: Early Chinese Trade in the South China Sea*. Singapore: Eastern Universities Press.

Wang, H. (2014). China's first empire? Interpreting the material record of the Erligang expansion. In K. Steinke & D. Ching, eds., *Art and Archaeology of the Erligang Civilization*. Princeton: Princeton University Press, pp. 67–97.

Wang, Y. (2003). Prehistoric walled settlements in the Chengdu Plain. *Journal of East Asian Archaeology*, 5(1–4), 109–48.

Wei, W. (2017). Yuenan jingnei Han mu de kaoguxue yanjiu [Archaeological Study of the Han Tombs in Vietnam]. PhD thesis, Jilin University.

Weng, Q. (2007). A historical perspective of river basin management in the Pearl River Delta of China. *Journal of Environmental Management*, 85, 1048–62.

Wengrow, D. (2010). *What Makes Civilization? The Ancient Near East and the Future of the West*. Oxford: Oxford University Press.

White, S. (2011). *The Climate of Rebellion in the Early Modern Ottoman Empire*. Cambridge: Cambridge University Press.

Wiens, H. (1954). *China's March toward the Tropics*. Hamden: The Shoe String Press.

Wu, D. (2022). The Bronze Economy and the Making of the Southern Borderlands under the Zhou Dynasty. PhD thesis, Columbia University.

Wu, X., Hein, A., Zhang, X., et al. (2019). Resettlement strategies and Han imperial expansion into Southwest China: A multimethod approach to colonialism and migration. *Archaeological and Anthropological Sciences*, 11, 6751–81.

Xiang, T. (2011). Erlitou wenhua xiang nanfang de chuanbo [Southward expansion of the Erlitou Culture]. *Kaogu*, 10, 47–61.

Xie, L., Lu, X., Sun, G., & Huang, W. (2017). Functionality and morphology: Identifying *si* agricultural tools from among Hemudu scapular implements in Eastern China. *Journal of Archaeological Method and Theory*, 24, 377–23.

Xin, D. (2013). Beijing daxue cang Qin shuilu licheng jiance chubu yanjiu [A preliminary study of the Qin mileage chart on bamboo slips from the Peking University collection]. *Chutu wenxian*, 4, 177–279.

Xu, J. (2006). Defining archaeological cultures at the Sanxingdui site. *Journal of East Asian Archaeology*, 5, 149–90.

Xu, H. (2017). *Xian Qin chengyi kaogu* [*Archaeology of Pre-Qin Cities*]. Beijing: Xiyuan.

Yang, B. (2019). *Cowrie Shells and Cowrie Money: A Global History*. London: Routledge.

Yang, K. (2003). *Zhanguo shi* [*The History of the Warring States*]. Shanghai: Shanghai Renmin.

Yang, Q. (2000). *Chu wenhua* [*The Chu Culture*]. Beijing: Wenwu.

Yao, A. (2016). *The Ancient Highlands of Southwest China: From the Bronze Age to the Han Empire*. Oxford: Oxford University Press.

Yao, A. & Jiang, Z. (2012). Rediscovering the settlement system of the "Dian" kingdom, in Bronze Age Southern China. *Antiquity*, 86, 353–67.

Yasuda, Y. (2013a). Discovery of the Yangtze River civilization in China. In Y. Yasuda, ed., *Water Civilization: From Yangtze to Khmer Civilizations*. Tokyo: Springer, pp. 3–45.

Yasuda, Y. (2013b). Epilogue: The decline of civilization. In Y. Yasuda, ed., *Water Civilization: From Yangtze to Khmer Civilizations*. Tokyo: Springer, 459–64.

Yates, R. (2013). Reflections on the foundation of the Chinese empire in the light of newly discovered legal and related manuscripts. In K. Chen, ed., *Dongya kaoguxue de zaisi – Zhang Guangzhi xiansheng shishi shi zhounian jinian lunwenji* [*Rethinking East Asian Archaeology: A Memorial Essay Collection for the Tenth Anniversary of Kwang-chih Chang's Death*]. Taipei: Academia Sinica, pp. 473–506.

Yoffee, N. (2004). *Myths of the Archaic State: Evolution of the Earliest Cities, States, and Civilizations*. Cambridge: Cambridge University Press.

Yu, L. (2013). Ningxiang qingtong wenhua qiyuan zaitansuo [Concerning the origins of the bronze culture of Ningxiang County]. *Wenwu*, 6, 1–6.

Zeng, M., Ma, C., Zhu, C., et al. (2016). Influence of climate change on the evolution of ancient culture from 4500 to 3700 cal. yr BP in the Chengdu Plain, upper reaches of the Yangtze River, China. *Catena*, 147, 742–54.

Zhang, B., ed. (2015). *Liangzhu wenhua kehua fuhao* [*Engraved Signs of the Liangzhu Culture*]. Shanghai: Shanghai Renmin.

Zhang, C. (2013). The Qujialing-Shijiahe Culture in the Middle Yangzi River valley. In A. Underhill, ed., *A Companion to Chinese Archaeology*. Chichester: Wiley-Blackwell, pp. 510–34.

Zhang, C. (2020). Guanyu Panlongcheng de xingzhi [On the nature of Panlongcheng]. *Jianghan kaogu*, 6, 53–56.

Zhang, H., Cheng, H., Sinha, A., et al. (2021). Collapse of the Liangzhu and other Neolithic cultures in the lower Yangtze region in response to climate change. *Science Advances*, 7(48), 1–9.

Zhang, J. (1998). *Sanqian nian yiqing* [*Three Thousand Years of Disease*]. Nanchang: Jiangxi Gaoxiao.

Zhang, X., Wang, X., Wu, X., et al. (2018). Investigating human migration and horse-trading in Yelang through strontium isotope analysis of skeletons from Zhongshui sites, south-west China (1300 BC – AD 25). *Archaeometry*, 60, 157–70.

Zhao, D. (2022a). Sanxingdui jisi huodong de jiben jiagou: Shentan, shenmiao, jisikeng [The basic structure of sacrificial activities at Sanxingdui: Altars, shrines, sacrificial pits]. *Sichuan wenwu*, 5, 80–94.

Zhao, D. (2022b). Lüelun Sanxingdui wenhua yu Changjiang zhongyou gu wenhua de guanxi [On the relationship between Sanxingdui Culture and the ancient cultures of the Middle Yangzi valley]. *Jianghan kaogu*, 2, 140–44.

Zhao, H., Gao, X., Jiang, Y., et al. (2021). Radiocarbon-dating an early minting site: Emergence of standardized coinage in China. *Antiquity*, 95, 1161–78.

Zhao, S. (2014). *Xian Qin Qin Han shiqi Lingnan shehui yu wenhua kaosuo – yi kaoguxue wei shijiao* [*Inquiry into Lingnan Society and Culture during the Pre-Qin and Qin-Han Periods: An Archaeological Perspective*]. Guangzhou: Jinan Daxue.

Zheng, W. (2012). *Chu guo fengjun yanjiu* [*A Study of the Enfeoffed Lords of the State of Chu*]. Wuhan: Hubei Jiaoyu.

Zhu, P. (2010). *Chu wenhua de xijian – Chu guo jingying xibu de kaoguxue guancha* [*The Westward Spread of Chu Culture: Archaeological Perspective on the Chu Management of Its Western Periphery*]. Chengdu: Bashu Shushe.

Zhu, Z., Zhang, Q., & Wang, F. (2006). The Jinsha site: An introduction. *Journal of East Asian Archaeology*, 5 (1–4), 247–76.

Zhuang, Y., Ding, P., & French, C. (2014). Water management and agricultural intensification of rice farming at the late-Neolithic site of Maoshan, Lower Yangtze River, China. *The Holocene*, 24(5), 531–45.

Zou, Y. & Zhang, X. (2013). *Zhongguo lishi ziran dili* [*Natural Historical Geography of China*]. Beijing: Kexue.

Zürcher, E. (2013). Tidings from the south: Chinese court Buddhism and overseas relations in the fifth century. In J. Silk, ed., *Buddhism in China: Collected Papers of Erik Zürcher*. Leiden: Brill, pp. 585–607.

Cambridge Elements

Ancient East Asia

About the Series

Elements in Ancient East Asia contains multi-disciplinary contributions focusing on the history and culture of East Asia in ancient times. Its framework extends beyond anachronistic, nation-based conceptions of the past, following instead the contours of Asian sub-regions and their interconnections with each other. Within the series there are five thematic groups: 'Sources', which includes excavated texts and other new sources of data; 'Environments', exploring interaction zones of ancient East Asia and long-distance connections; 'Institutions', including the state and its military; 'People', including family, gender, class, and the individual and 'Ideas', concerning religion and philosophy, as well as the arts and sciences. The series presents the latest findings and strikingly new perspectives on the ancient world in East Asia.

Cambridge Elements

Ancient East Asia

Elements in the Series

A full series listing is available at: www.cambridge.org/EAEA

For EU product safety concerns, contact us at Calle de José Abascal, 56–1°, 28003 Madrid, Spain or eugpsr@cambridge.org.

www.ingramcontent.com/pod-product-compliance
Ingram Content Group UK Ltd.
Pitfield, Milton Keynes, MK11 3LW, UK
UKHW022146080726
473066UK00010B/802

* 9 7 8 1 1 0 8 9 6 4 6 7 8 *